PARENTS

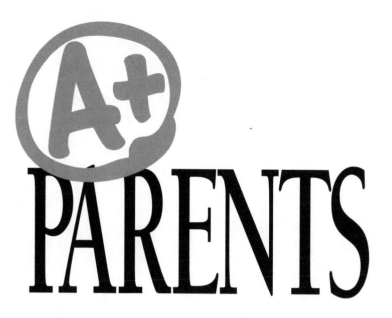

PARENTS

Help Your Child Learn and Succeed in School

by Adrienne Mack

McBOOKS PRESS
ITHACA, NEW YORK

Book and cover design by Anne Kilgore. Illustrations by Susan MacKay.

Library of Congress Cataloging-in-Publication Data

Mack, Adrienne, 1944–
    A+ parents : help your child learn and succeed in school / by Adrienne Mack.
        p.   cm.
    Includes bibliographical references and index.
    ISBN 0-935526-36-6 (pbk.)
    1. Education—Parent participation. 2. Study skills. 3. Home and school. 4. Readiness for school. 5. Child rearing. I. Title.
    LB1048.5M33 1997   97-3145
    370. 19'2—dc21   CIP

Additional copies of this book and other McBooks Press titles may be ordered from any bookstore or directly from McBooks Press, 120 West State Street, Ithaca, NY 14850. Please include $3 postage and handling for mail orders. New York State residents must add 8% sales tax. All McBooks Press publications can also be ordered by calling toll-free, 1-888-266-5711.

Visit our website: http://www.mcbooks.com.

Distributed to the book trade by:
Login Trade
1436 West Randolph Street
Chicago, IL 60607
1-800-243-0138; fax 1-800-334-3892

Printed in the United States of America

9 8 7 6 5 4 3 2 1

For my husband, five children, grandchildren, and the thousands of students and parents who taught me, and continue to teach me, all I know about parenting.

CONTENTS

INTRODUCTION   9

PART I: *The Home Environment*

    CHAPTER 1: Getting Your Preschooler Ready to Learn   13

       Take a Personal Inventory • Understanding the
Nature of the Child • Tender Loving Care • Mealtime
• Respect • Discipline • Time-Outs are for Everyone •
Words to Avoid • Magic Words • Random Acts of
Kindness • Child Care Away From Home • Chores
and Responsibility • Working and Playing with
Others • Toys and Playtime

    CHAPTER 2: Organization and Routines   46

       Same Old Time, Same Old Place • Bedtime •
School Clothes • A Place for Everything • Long-
and Short-Term Projects

PART II: *The Basics*

    CHAPTER 3: Reading   55

       Getting Ready to Read • The Spoken Word •
Reading Aloud • Real-World Reading • Selecting
Books • Reading in School • Reading Ideas

    CHAPTER 4: Writing   69

       Getting Ready to Write • Helping Your Child Once
School Starts • Writing Ideas

CHAPTER 5: Math   76

     Getting Ready to Do Math • Helping Your Child
     Once School Starts • Math Ideas

PART III: *School and Beyond*

    CHAPTER 6: School Days   85

     Fed, Clothed, and Equipped • Attendance •
     Medical Care and Emergency Information • School
     Rules and Behavior • Multiculturalism and
     Difference • There are Some Lemons on Every Staff
     • Getting to Know the School • Helping Your Child
     Stand Out in a Crowd • Report Cards and Grades •
     Self-Assessment and School Portfolios

    CHAPTER 7: Homework   109

     Responsibility • A Quiet Place • Study Time •
     Assistance

    CHAPTER 8: Multimedia   116

     Television • Movies and Videos • Radio • Home
     Computers • Video and Computer Games

    CHAPTER 9: Outings, Trips, and Adventures   129

CONCLUSION   135

RECOMMENDED READING   137

INDEX   140

INTRODUCTION

BEING A parent[1] is a tough job. We are responsible for the well-being of another life. We want our children to be happy, healthy, successful. We want to take care of them so well, that one day they will know how to take good care of themselves. A successful child doesn't have to be a genius. Nor should she[2] be measured by the same standards used for adults. A successful child has enough faith in herself to take risks, try new challenges, and work up to her capability. She is developing a set of personal standards, a code of ethics, a sense of responsibility, sensitivity, independence, and proper behavior. Most of all, a successful child is someone who is learning how to learn, and who will continue to learn throughout her life.

A+ Parents: Help Your Child Learn and Succeed in School is a sensible, friendly guide to the best parenting practices for raising successful children in the early years. You don't have

---

1 The term "parent" refers to a male or female parent, guardian, grandparent, baby-sitter, and/or any caregiver in a position to be with the child for all or part of the time.

2 To avoid the cumbersome use of "he/she," the chapters alternate between using the male pronoun and the female pronoun. Each section is intended for all children, boys and girls, as well as for adults of both sexes.

to be a Ph.D. to understand these techniques, or a stay-at-home parent to carry them out. The book is designed to show you how to help your child achieve the goals you value. Whether you begin with chapter one or open to any page at random, you'll find practical steps to raising successful children that you can apply *right now.*

Each section is written to encourage thinking about children, reinforce what you already know, encourage you when you might need encouragement, remind you of techniques that work, and inform you of what you may not already know. Although I urge you to pay particular attention to providing a home environment that fosters learning, every family is unique. Take from these pages what works for you and your family and feel free to set aside the rest.

Children in the 4-to-8 age group will benefit most from the ideas presented in this book, but many of the concepts apply equally well to children from birth to age 12 and beyond. Don't worry if you are just now realizing that your child needs more help from you. The techniques offered in this handbook can be used right now, with any child. Begin where you are without wasting time lamenting past mistakes or inconsistencies in your child-rearing approach. Guilt over past performance doesn't get us any closer to achieving the goal of raising successful children. Begin today and do what you can. Children are amazingly resilient. With caring and supportive behavior on your part, your children will learn, and they will succeed.

PART I:
The Home Environment

Chapter 1

GETTING YOUR PRESCHOOLER READY TO LEARN

FOR THE most part, children who are successful in school, and who know how to apply what they have learned, come from homes that value education. Those homes send their kids off to school with an attitude that says, "Learn all you can. What you do is important. Participate; get involved." Not even the best education program, or series of programs, can take the place of a home where the message is: "Get educated; we'll do everything within our power to help."

Before you can expect much from your child, you need to create a climate at home that encourages success. The task can be daunting, but the success your child achieves is well worth the effort. Your child's future success begins with you.

TAKE A PERSONAL INVENTORY

Are you the kind of person you want your child to be? You're his role model. Kids do what you do. If you enjoy learning, so will your child. If you read, your child will. Unfortunately, our children are just as likely to pick up our bad habits as our good ones. If you yell and hit, there's a strong likelihood your child will yell and hit. What you do, what you say, what you praise and encourage him for doing is what your child will learn is good. It's what he will value.

Caring for your children teaches them to care for others, and for themselves. A child also picks up any tension that exists among the adults in his life. It's been said that the best thing a father can do for his children is to love their mother. Any loving variation on that theme to include different family structures also works.

If you're not the person you want your child to be, it's time you became that person. As your child develops, so will you. No one told you raising a child would be easy, but you can do it, and do it well. As you work at becoming a better parent, don't be surprised if you become a better person.

UNDERSTANDING THE NATURE OF THE CHILD Children are unique beings, not just miniature adults. They come to you with a blank slate waiting to absorb everything the world has to offer. In a remarkably short period of time, a newborn learns to crawl, then walk, then talk. Three months' growth in infancy equals the intellectual development of the period from 4 to 17 years. Appropriate stimulation during this time can help develop a child's intelligence. Understanding how children learn is a key to helping them develop.

Children are naturally curious and crave stimulation. They learn through experiencing the world. During infancy, a child's room should be brightly colored, providing lots of interesting images for him to absorb. There should be soft things for him to touch, and rattles for him to shake. Talking and singing to your child is also stimulating and soothing. A tape deck softly playing Mozart works well, too. (Researchers are finding that children who listen to classical music tend to have an easier time learning mathematics and science. The patterns the brain establishes for listening are the same ones needed to process math.)

Experimentation is a natural part of every child. As the infant matures, he continues to want to try everything. Putting on your makeup, pouring oil on the garage floor, pulling all the pans out of the cupboard—or handling the gun you left lying around—are not things he does just to vex you. Children want to touch everything they see because they are trying to learn about the world they live in. They are curious, and everything from the benign to the dangerous is interesting to them.

Encourage your child's uniqueness: "That's an interesting way of doing _____. Show me how you did it." Constant criticism can diminish a child's confidence and inhibit his creativity. Allow him to experiment.

Children don't sit still well, at least not for long periods of time. They need to be on the go, to get up and move around. They are not good at keeping quiet. Limit the times you put the very young child in an environment where he has to sit still and be very quiet. He will learn how to sit still and be quiet as he grows older. For a two-year-old, begin with a minute or two, then add a few more minutes at a time.

Children need the freedom to talk. By age two they are holding conversations—even if you don't understand them. By three a child has a vocabulary of many hundreds of words and acquires new ones every day. Children who are always told to "shut up" lose their inquisitiveness. They become the ones who never ask questions in the classroom. They have learned not to.

Young kids are very self-centered. Their stories are full of themselves: "I have a doll." "I went on a walk." "Me. Me. Me." They explore their world from the center out. Don't worry about their apparent selfishness. Well-balanced children do develop an awareness and sensitivity to others, but it takes time.

Children love to be around people, but only in small groups. Masses of people can be overwhelming. Even the most outgoing kid may cling to your trouser leg at the family reunion or in church. The presence of so many adults can make them feel very small and insignificant. It's amazing what the addition of another "little person" can do to make the scared child feel safe and happy again. No one available? Squat down when you talk to your child. Come down to his level.

Children get cranky when they are overstimulated or if the setting is confusing. Too many new people, new experiences, and too much activity can lead to a whining child. Kids need some space and time alone, but that doesn't mean they have to be stuck in a playpen, or closed away in their bedroom. "Alone space" can be created in the center of the family room. Try spreading a sheet over a table. Leave one side up and let the sheet close off the other three sides creating a tent-like space for him beneath. Your child may want to pull the fourth side down as well, but let him decide.

Kids also need a space where they can make the rules and be in charge. Playtime is crucial because it allows children to explore and learn through self-initiated activity. In addition to fostering creativity, playing with others is also excellent preparation for working with others. Regularly provide your child with ample playtime.

Children want to do for themselves as early as possible. "Don't help me" really means "Help me to do it myself."

There are times when you'll feel terribly impatient and want to pick up his toys yourself, button his sweater, or even feed him when he's indicated he wants to feed himself. Whenever possible, slow down, watch and assist, but let him do as much as he is capable of doing. Trust him to get the job done, even though it won't be done as well or as quickly as you can do it.

Kids have poor coordination. They drop, spill, and fumble. A harsh word may make them drop, spill, and fumble even more. Give them time; they'll get it right.

Constant frustration is a part of childhood. There is so much a child can't reach, do, see, or accomplish. But small achievements—especially if praised—can mean a lot. Depending on the child's age, he can take pride in a new way of stacking blocks, helping to put the groceries away, or learning to ride a tricycle or bicycle. Children want to be successful, just as we all do. Help them achieve small successes, building one success on another.

Children want to please you. Recognize their efforts and don't forget to say "thank you."

TENDER LOVING CARE

The first step to having a successful, well-adjusted child is a daily dose of TLC. Children thrive when they know they are loved. They can think better, they behave themselves, and they're a lot happier.

Childhood is the time when children learn what big people are all about. Are they safe? Can they be trusted? Will they love me? During the first six years, children are learning to love themselves. They won't learn to love themselves if they don't feel loved by others.

Children with affectionate parents have a much better

chance of growing up emotionally sound. No matter how busy your schedule, make time to fit a little TLC into each day.

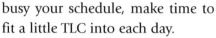

Here are some suggestions:

◆ Begin every day with a hug, a smile, a cuddle, or a "huggle" (several family members joining in a group hug). Find out what your child likes best. Some prefer a squeeze, a tickle (but not if the child screams to stop), a back rub, a kiss on the nose. Rubbing noses makes most children laugh. Be affectionate in ways that feel comfortable to you and your child.

◆ Establish a secret gesture that means "I love you," a sign just between the two of you, or something your young child can imitate and repeat: rolling the eyes, pulling on an ear, wrinkling the nose or touching its tip with your pinky. You can be talking on the phone, cooking dinner, standing in a crowded room, or rushing out the door, and still send a loving signal to your child. Send the signal even when others are around. Establish a different secret signal for each child. Make it truly special.

◆ Take the time to say, "I'm crazy about you," or "I'm so lucky to be your mom/dad," or "I'm glad you're here for me to take care of."

◆ Start your day ten minutes earlier. I can hear the groans now, but it's worth a try. The payoffs are bigger than any you might win in the lottery. Find out how your child would like to spend the ten morning minutes, then do it. Be prepared to change the nature of these ten minutes as your child grows. It could be something as simple as getting the morning paper together or letting the dog out for his constitutional. You could use the minutes to cuddle with your kids in bed, to read a short story, to plan the day, or even, if you must, to give instructions. Before you give your time and energy to anyone or anything else, give your best to your child. The message you'll be relaying is: "You're important."

MEALTIME

Children can't learn if their stomachs are growling. Too many children come to school hungry.

A bowl of oatmeal is quick, nutritious, and costs only pennies. Or be innovative if you don't have "traditional" breakfast foods on hand. Who says you can only serve peanut butter and jelly for lunch? A sandwich, a glass of milk, and a piece of fruit works for breakfast. Even last night's leftovers, if they're put on a plate and reheated, can be a nutritious start for the day.

Don't set food down in front of your child and walk away. If at all possible, sit down and have breakfast with him. If you're pressed for time, at least stay in the kitchen while you finish dressing, or use the time to put last night's dishes away. As you move about, stay where your child can see you. Ask about what's going to happen today at school, at the baby-sitter's, or at home. Talk helps establish a bond which will make your child feel loved and secure.

I firmly believe that the single most important thing my husband and I did as parents was insist that the family eat dinner together nearly every night. It was around the table that we shared news of the day, kept in touch with ongoing events, talked about successes and failures, and discussed world events. We laughed together, had more than one food fight, and even though a kid occasionally left the table in tears from too much teasing, we resolved many problems and disagreements. Sharing meals was our way of sharing the ups and the downs of our lives.

No matter how busy the day (my husband and I were actively involved in our careers, and the children had many after-school activities and later, part-time jobs), we came together to share a meal. The daily contact didn't allow our kids to slip too far away from us or to get into activities that we didn't approve of.

I believe that the "destruction of the American family" can be traced more to TV trays than to single-parent homes. When I've surveyed my students, at all grade levels, those who were not successful had many things in common. One thing which stood out was that they didn't eat dinner together as a family. If the household consists of one adult and one child, then that's the family. If there are two parents and five kids, then that's the family. No matter what the circumstances, dinnertime, even if you're only able to manage it once a week, means a shared meal. It doesn't have to be a feast, but it is very important that you have it together.

Here are some tips for making the most of your family mealtimes:

◆ No television during dinner. No exceptions. This might be even more difficult than finding the time to eat together. Sharing a meal while watching reruns of "Married With Children" will not bring the family closer together or help your child to be more successful.

◆ Allow for a break. Very young children should not be expected to sit through a long dinner. Before the meal, show your child where the salt and pepper shakers, the butter, or the extra bread are kept. Then, when he gets restless, ask him to go get one of those items. He'll feel important, be able to stretch, and be prepared to sit again.

◆ Have a conversation. Meals are not about giving orders for the week, scolding the children for not doing their chores, or passing "meaningful" glances at your mate. Conversation is also not "Pass the peas," "I don't like spinach," or "This is good."

Talk about your day, what you did, who you saw. Tell about grandpa or your boss. If all else fails, describe the contents of the mail or discuss what's in the news. Rose Kennedy used to assign news articles to her children which they were to share with the family at dinner. Dinner-table conversation was lively and informative. She fed their minds while she fed their bodies. You can, too.

However, meaningful conversation doesn't have to be about world politics. Ask your child to talk about his day. Even the young child will enjoy telling you about a truck he saw pass in the street or what he found on his walk around the block. Try a variation of the Kennedy method. Ask your child in advance, when he's old enough to remember (over three), to tell you a story during dinner. You might suggest a topic like "our trip to the supermarket," "my favorite thing to do at preschool," or "a funny kid in school." Make his story the center of your conversation, even if only for five minutes.

Dinner conversation is important for children of all ages. The very young child won't be part of your conversation, but he's absorbing language all the time. By two he'll be joining the conversation, even if you can't understand him. By three he'll be participating with his own stories.

If your child is monopolizing the conversation, don't say "shut up," but do set limits. "Estella, I loved your story about _____, but now Daddy's going to have a turn, and you can be the listener." Keep in mind that even a minute of sitting still and listening can seem like a long time to a young child.

Young children love to talk. It's only as they get older that they begin to give one-word answers: "What did you do in school today?" "Nothing." When this begins to happen, or if it already has, switch to open-ended questions or comments: "How did you and _____ work out the problem you told us about last week?" "I'm interested to hear about the games you played at the baby-sitter's house." You may also keep the story going by asking "What happened next?" or "What do you think might happen tomorrow?"

Listen to what your children are saying. Sometimes, as he tells you about his activities, a child will reveal a problem, situation, or even a hope or aspiration you didn't know he had. Paying attention, being sensitive, and responding to what your child says will help build a strong bond of confidence between the two of you.

If you have established the routine of eating dinner together, you'll have more open communication with your child as he gets older. The better your communication, the more faith you can have that your child is making the right decisions. Teenagers who regularly talk to their parents are less likely to get involved with things they wouldn't want to talk about (e.g., drugs, poor choices of friends, failing grades).

The benefits of sharing meals together on a regular basis are many. In addition to bonding families, listening to stories and telling their own helps young children learn about sequencing events, and about beginnings, middles, and ends. Kids learn about predicting what might happen in the future, and about listening and responding. All are important skills for reading and writing.

RESPECT

To respect someone is to show consideration, to honor them as a person, to treat them with courtesy. All of us respond better to others when we are treated with respect, when our privacy of space, possessions, and body are not violated. When children are raised in a respectful environment, they bring that same respect to their dealings with others. We teach our children respect not by demanding it, but by modeling it. Children mimic what they see.

Mutual respect between a parent and a child is crucial. Respect your children and they will learn to respect you. They're not likely to treat you, or anyone, with any more or any less respect than you show toward them. Talk to them in a way that shows you believe in them and their ability to do things well.

Not: "How could you be so careless!"

But: "Next time, when you want something on the other side of the table, please ask for it to be passed. That way we'll avoid spills."

Before you speak to your child in anger, ask yourself if you would say that to your neighbor or your boss. If you wouldn't talk to another adult in that tone of voice, don't talk to your child like that.

Respect a child's body. Don't touch your child anywhere that makes him feel uncomfortable. When he announces or indicates that he wants to go to the bathroom by himself, bathe himself (safely), or dry himself, it's time to allow him to do that. Knock before entering the bathroom or his bedroom. Ask, "May I come in?" Teach him that closed doors mean privacy, and respect his. He'll respect yours in return.

Respect a child's belongings and private space. We each need a place to call our own. Your children may have their own room or may share sleeping quarters with one or more siblings, or with extended family members. The more crowded the living conditions, the more important it is for a child to have a space that is his alone. A shoe box with a lid can suffice, as can a dresser drawer, or a blanket box slid away under the bed. What is most important is that the child knows the space is his and that no one will violate it, not even you. This teaches the child to respect other people's belongings as well, including yours.

Having a space of his own, and respecting other people's space, will prepare your child for having his own desk at school and for respecting his neighbor's desk, crayons, and notebook.

DISCIPLINE

Children don't come with an inborn sense of right and wrong. They have to be taught. Raising our kids to know the difference between good and bad is challenging. Discipline can help us instill good values in our children.

The goal of discipline is to discourage inappropriate behavior and replace it with appropriate behavior. In order for your children to get a clear sense of what this means, they need to trust you. It is also important to remember that discipline works best when it is used sparingly.

Here are some basic rules to guide you:

- ◆ Decide what's important to you.
- ◆ Set a good example.
- ◆ Set reasonable boundaries and expectations.
- ◆ Reward good behavior and rechannel negative behavior.
- ◆ Be consistent and persistent.
- ◆ Be firm but fair.
- ◆ Explain the reason for the rules.
- ◆ Wait for tempers to cool—even yours!

Decide what's important to you, not to your neighbor or your child's teacher. If you don't mind your kid getting dirty, don't make staying clean a rule. Pick what values you want to emphasize, and make sure your behavior reflects them.

The best thing you can do to assure your children have a clear sense of right and wrong is to set a good example. Children want to do what you do. "Do what I say and not what I do" is a mixed message that confuses children and sets them up to disappoint you. There's nothing wrong with an adult having a beer and explaining it away with "Adults get to do some things that children aren't able to. I know right now this seems very unfair, but someday you'll understand." If the child trusts the adult, he will accept that explanation. But don't overuse it.

Create a setting where it's easy for kids to behave well. That does not mean everything and anything goes. Put latches on closets and drawers you don't want a young child to get into, but leave at least one closet open with things he can play with. You can also store your plastic bowls and storage containers on lower shelves for your child to play with.

Set reasonable boundaries. By age three children can distinguish between what they can get into and what they can't. It's okay to make certain areas of the house off limits. If you don't want your child to romp on your best furniture in the living room, that's fine. But not if you also put the dining room, bedroom, garage, and so on off limits. Excluding him from too many places sends the message that he's not wanted.

Set limits early, then be ready to change them as the family and child change. Don't be afraid of trial and error. If a rule stops working for you or your child, drop it and tell your child why.

Reward good behavior to help build a warm, loving environment. Some children act out because that's the only way they can get attention. Rewarding good behavior discourages this. "Alice, I really liked how you shared your toys with Maria," or "When you put your toys away, I have more time to play with you. Thank you for your help." A kind word, a smile, or a hug are all great rewards. They are not time-consuming nor do they cost anything.

Rechannel negative behavior. Young children are easily distracted. If your child is displaying a behavior you want to discourage, present him with an alternative. For instance, when he bangs on the table with a spoon, give him an empty oatmeal box or a set of plastic bowls to bang on instead. You can also try diverting the banging to a toy piano, or if the noise has become too much, set out a doll, some building blocks, or another favorite toy.

Be consistent and persistent. Children don't all learn the difference between good and bad behavior in the same way, or at the same speed. For some youngsters, one correction is enough. For most, a dozen is not enough. If there's a behavior you wish to change (running across the street, throwing toys at other children, shouting to get your attention), responding to the behavior each time your child exhibits it will get the point across.

Children don't always get it. They don't automatically apply a rule they learned at home to a new setting outside the home. New setting equals new rules. When going into a new environment, go over the rules. For example, before shopping talk about *store voices* and how they are lower than *play voices*. Discuss the rules about touching things in the store. Set rewards for "not touching" and let your child touch some things: the smooth silk of lingerie, a stuffed animal, a box of cereal, etc.

Be firm but fair. You don't have to correct everything your child does. If he wants to eat peas with his fingers while he's learning to use a fork, let it be. If he prefers to put his shoes under the bed when you want them in the closet, let it go. If he insists on wearing a shirt and pants that don't match, or two socks that are different colors, it's okay. Save your energy for more important battles.

Don't set your child up for failure. Trying to correct too much at once can overwhelm him. If you want to work on respecting others' property, wait before you work on table manners.

Have reasonable expectations. Taking the young child to a fancy restaurant where he can't move around, then expecting him to sit through a long meal, is an unreasonable expectation. Ask yourself: Is this setting appropriate for my child? What will he be doing while I visit with a neighbor (or go to the market or have a quiet dinner with my spouse)? Planning ahead can save a lot of aggravation. When you do need to bring the kids along on a tedious errand, keep the trip short.

Going to the mall may be fun for you, but young children don't understand shopping for clothes for three hours—especially when they cannot touch everything that interests them. Plan breaks for food, for running around, for playing. A trip to the grocery story can be an adventure if they are allowed to put groceries in the basket, are consulted about some of the things you are buying, or get to choose some of their favorite foods. If you can, save your long shopping trips for when you can go without the children. Exchange baby-sitting time with a neighbor, spouse, or relative.

Explain the reason for the rules. Depending on a child's age and level of development, it will make it easier for him to remember and respect a rule if he understands it. "I don't want you to open the kitchen drawers because the sharp knives inside could hurt you." "Brother doesn't want anybody to go in his room when he's not home. That's his private place." "Holding my hand when we cross the street is a good idea so we don't lose one another and get in the way of the cars." "We don't talk when others are talking so that everyone gets a turn. You'll have a turn after _____."

In order to be consistent, fair, and reasonable, it is important not to make so many rules you have trouble keeping track of them. Rules you aren't prepared to keep and punishments so complicated or severe you won't be able to carry them out will confuse your child, making it difficult for him to behave well.

Save "because I say so" for those times when your patience has absolutely run dry—it will. When possible, explain why you want the child to change his behavior. At the dinner table, you may be able to quiet your child with, "When you speak loudly no one else is able to hear," or "I can hear you better when you ask nicely. Shouting hurts my ears." When you want your child to sit still in a restaurant, you could explain, "If you run around, the waiter may trip over you and spill all the hot food."

Children don't always deliberately break a rule. Talk through the behavior whenever possible: "Why did you throw the green beans on the floor?"

"Because I don't like them."

"Next time you don't like something, tell me. Maybe we can exchange it for something else."

The second time it happens you might say, "Do you remember when you threw down the green beans and I told you not to throw food on the floor? Now you'll have to pick them up."

It might take longer for you to supervise his green bean pick-up than it would for you to pick them up yourself, but he'll never learn if you keep picking up after him. Remember: "Let the punishment fit the crime."

Match discipline to the behavior. If you punish your child when he spills a glass of milk, what will you do when he finger-paints your couch or hits his baby brother? Some transgressions are worse than others and should be treated accordingly. Beating your child, however, is never appropriate. If his behavior makes you so angry you don't think you can discipline him properly, put the child in another room or in someone else's care to give each of you some time out.

No matter what, don't humiliate your child. Whenever possible, try disciplining in private. Take him aside, away from other eyes and ears. Kneel down to his level. Look at your child and speak quietly but firmly. Suggest an appropriate behavior to take the place of the inappropriate one.

When a situation results in anger, wait for tempers to cool, then go over what happened. Have the child list the events.

You might begin, "When you wanted to play with Andrea's doll, what did you do?" Lead the child through the events providing alternative choices. Check often for understanding.

"How did you feel when Andrea wouldn't let you play with her doll?" Help your child to acknowledge his feelings.

"What else could you have done besides grabbing the doll away or hitting Andrea?" Help your child develop some alternative strategies.

Sometimes the best we can do is let our children know that we don't always get what we want. Life doesn't always seem fair. Maybe next time it will be different, maybe not. Maybe Andrea won't ever want to share.

Through discipline, children learn that consequences derive from actions. If your child always hits other children, he won't have any friends. If he consistently throws food on the floor, he'll spend a lot of time cleaning it up. If he doesn't help put his toys away, he won't have any toys to play with. Explaining the consequences of your child's actions, and helping him to understand the concept, will greatly help him to be successful. He will come to understand that some behaviors lead to rewards and feeling good, while other behaviors lead to punishments and feeling bad.

TIME-OUTS ARE FOR EVERYONE

A time-out is just what it sounds like: a time away from whatever is happening. It is an opportunity to regroup, to regain control of oneself. It's a period of renewal. By taking some time away from the situation, we give ourselves and our children time to reflect and to consider appropriate actions. Time-outs help children build inner discipline, gain control of themselves, and think before reacting.

How will time-outs help your child be more successful in school? Teachers use time-outs in class, especially in the very early grades. If your child understands time-outs, he will be more easily socialized to the classroom environment. He will accept his own need for a time-out and will understand when others are given a time-out.

Adults as well as children can benefit from time-outs. If you've had a hard day and you need a little time between work and home, tell the kids you're going to have a time-out. If possible, go into another room. If not, you might want to wear something, such as a baseball cap in a loud color, which announces to the rest of the family that you're taking a time-out. Sit on the couch and open mail, read the paper, meditate. Insist your child respect your private time, even if you are in the same room. "I've had a hard day today. I'd like to tell you about it, but first I need to take a time-out for fifteen minutes." An automatic timer, the kind commonly used in the kitchen, is an excellent visual way for children to understand how long the time-out will be.

Feeling angry and ready to hit your child? Take a time-out. "I'm really angry now. I need to have a time-out for five minutes. We'll talk about this then." Or: "We're both very upset. It's time for both of us to have a time-out." Time-outs allow you to defuse the situation before it escalates.

Separating children to different corners of the room, or to different rooms, can cool an explosive situation. "If you can't get along nicely and share your toys, then it's time for you to stop playing together. For the next ten minutes (set the timer) you may not talk to one another. You'll be on different sides of the room." This was one of my mother's favorite techniques. Funny how separating two quarreling children frequently leads to them becoming the best of friends!

As with other forms of discipline, you need to be consistent with time-outs. Decide what situations warrant their use, and then follow through. For example, if you are in the grocery store with a screaming toddler, you might consider a time-out. Tell the grocery clerk that you'll be leaving the store for a few minutes, and ask him to set your cart aside. Then take your toddler outside. "We're going to stay outside for five minutes. When you're ready to behave, we can continue our shopping." You might think of it as a great inconvenience to yourself, but standing outside the grocery store for five minutes is much preferred to pushing a shopping cart with a screaming toddler down the grocery aisles.

Time-outs can be used for disciplining children, but often time-outs, for ourselves or our children, are appropriate when we're sleepy, angry, need some time to think, can't figure out how to share, are fighting with friends, siblings, our spouse, and so on. Time-outs are for anyone and everyone, whenever a break is needed.

WORDS TO AVOID

At best, raising children is stressful. When you add a job, running a household, paying bills, and the rest of life's demands into the equation, raising successful children seems downright impossible. The demands of each day can be overwhelming and frustrating, making our children easy targets for our anger. We need to remind ourselves that our children deserve the best of us, not the worst. If we send our best to them, we are more likely to get their best in return.

The things you say to your children are important to them. They are relying on you for guidance, encouragement, and confidence. You won't get very far asking questions that begin with "Why can't you _____?" or "Why don't you _____?" The reality is kids don't know why they do what they do. They react by instinct until you teach them differently. That's what socialization is all about. If you load your comments and criticisms with negativity, they may never learn the right way to do something.

Don't say things like: "Why must you always pick at your food?" Try: "You know, when you eat very slowly I have to spend more time in the kitchen and I have less time to play with you," or "It's okay if you want to eat slowly, but I can only sit at the table with you for another five minutes. Then I have to clean the kitchen." Set the timer if necessary.

Hurtful words can permanently scar your child. Never say: "I wish you were never born." Remind your child that: "You are a great gift to me (us). I'm so happy you're here!"

Don't compare your children to one another or to the kid down the block, at least not where they can hear you. I can't think of anything that troubles children more than being compared to their siblings, especially if the sibling truly is more beautiful/handsome, brilliant, talented, well-liked, and so on. Each child is unique, with different talents and strengths. Make sure your child feels special.

Don't make promises you can't keep. Children learn to trust other adults by how well they learn to trust you. Don't say: "Sure we'll go to Disneyland someday," if you know it's unlikely. Instead you might say: "I'd love to take you to Disneyland. It would be a lot of fun, but we just can't do that right now." You needn't apologize for things you can't afford. Kids don't have to have $100 sneakers to fit in. "I know you'd love to have those _____, but we can't buy (do) that."

Avoid saying: "I'll make it all better." You can't always make it better, nor should you. Learning how to cope with disappointments is an important part of life. Allow your child to be sad or mad for awhile when a disappointment comes along. Listen and sympathize with your child: "I know you were really counting on _____. You must be feeling very _____." Don't take the child's pain away with your own story: "When I was your age I didn't get to go to _____ either." Allow the child to have his own feelings, at least for the moment.

Don't battle with your kids. Instead of: "I've told you a dozen times and I'm not going to tell you again. You'd better clean up this mess." Try: "It's time to clean up the toys. Let's set the timer. You decide how long it will take you to pick up the toys. When you're all done we can go to the park together (or read a story, play a game, etc.)." If you encounter resistance, change the approach: "I told you that it was time to pick up the toys. You still haven't done it. Now I will pick them up, but there won't be time for us to go to the park." Actions have consequences. Make the consequences real.

Expect your child to do well. Tell him he can be successful in school. Families who expect more from their children get more. Success has much more to do with effort than with ability. It's also never too early to talk to your child about college or training after high school. When our children were growing up, a typical dinner table conversation was not about *if* they would go, but *where* they would go to college.

MAGIC WORDS   "Please." "Thank you." "Excuse me." "I'm sorry." "May I have a turn?" "Can I play?" "I don't understand. Say that again, please." These are the words that make people like us, that give us a chance to try something, and that help us achieve what we want. These are the "magic words" that will help build success.

Magic words are not just for strangers. Use them regularly at home and insist your child use them too. Polite children are appreciated and rewarded in school. Teachers often believe that when a child displays good manners he comes from a home with caring parents. When a teacher knows a parent cares, he will give more time to helping the child, knowing that his help will be reinforced at home.

Magic words are more than polite expressions. They reflect strong values. Children who begin school without good manners are already behind. They have lessons to learn, some of them harsh ones, before they can get down to the business of reading, writing, and arithmetic. If your child knows how to treat people nicely and how to work well with others, school will be a much more productive experience for him. Excusing your child's poor manners or selfish ways on the grounds that "he'll grow out of it" may doom your child to be unliked and unsuccessful in school and in later life.

RANDOM ACTS OF KINDNESS

One of our goals as parents is to raise generous children. Children are naturally selfish until they are taught to share. Teaching them to be generous will make them feel good, raise their self-esteem, and instill pride and joy in them. In addition, if your child enters school already knowing how to share, he will be well on the road to success. Learning to share is extremely important because it is the key to working well with others. Once in school, your child will work in small groups on a daily basis.

The best way to teach is by example. Show your child what it means to share: "This is my favorite ice cream. Let's share it." "May I play with your blocks with you?" "You may have the _____ for five minutes, then it's _____'s turn." Use the automatic timer if necessary.

Invite your child's playmate over for lunch or an after-nap/after-school snack. For dessert have them share a treat. Here's an approach my mother used for us: one child divides the treat, the other gets to choose his piece first. Trust me, they will do everything they can to divide evenly.

Emphasize that sharing is give and take. Provide opportunities for your child to be the giver. "May I please have some of your _____?" "I think Grandma would be happy to have a picture from you." "Perhaps you can help me write a letter to Grandpa." Show your child that generosity is giving, not self-serving.

Pack an extra treat in your child's lunchbox. Suggest he pick a friend at school to share the treat with. After school ask, "Did you enjoy your treat? Who did you share with? How did you feel when you shared it?" Don't be surprised if he says, "I wanted to eat it myself," or "I ate it myself." You say, "I know. Sometimes you want to keep all of the treats for yourself. But I hope sometimes you will share because then your friends will share with you."

Praise your child's generosity. "I saw that you gave Margaret your shovel to use. How nice of you to share your things with her." "I'm sure some other little boy or girl will be happy to play with the _____ you are giving to charity."

Do community service with your child. As a family, serve a meal at a mission, pour coffee and cookies at a community function, volunteer at the library, pick up trash in the park, or encourage your child to donate used clothing to a shelter. Instilling volunteerism in your child will help him feel important and like he can make a difference.

CHILD CARE AWAY FROM HOME

The decision to leave your children in someone else's care is a momentous one, not to be taken lightly. Many parents have no choice but to rely on others. They need to work to make ends meet, or have such a compelling career that to abandon it would make them miserable. Whatever the reason, once you've made the decision, lay the guilt aside. Guilt doesn't help. Even with limited time, there's much you can do to help your child be successful and feel loved.

Select your caregiver carefully. Although it may be very tempting and easy to leave your child in the care of a neighbor, friend, or relative who is home with several other children, remember that the person you choose will have a great impact on the upbringing and welfare of your child.

Don't be afraid to interview the caregiver. You need to know more than the cost. Ask about their education. Have they studied child development? What do they know about a child's need for a rich language environment? It is not enough that the caregiver says, "I do this because I love children." You certainly hope they do, but they must also be aware of how children learn and what kind of environment they need. The caregiver you want for your child should be educated.

If you must choose a caregiver who is not very educated, then it is your responsibility to help educate him. For instance, if he has no books for the children, get some from the library and give instructions that he read to your child every day. Then ask if he did.

When selecting a child care facility, spend some time there first. Check out the child-to-adult ratio. As a simple guideline, there should be no more than three infants to one adult, four toddlers to one adult, or six preschoolers to one adult. Look for an active environment: children moving about exploring, touching, playing. Look to see if there are books available and ask if the caregiver reads to the children on a daily basis. Check out the toys. They should be accessible, age-appropriate, safe, and varied. Beware environments where children are placed in playpens and left alone for much of the day. Although they may be safe, a playpen environment is not very stimulating and tends to isolate the child. If you're choosing to leave your child in a private home, be suspicious if there's a television in the playroom. Too many private child care providers use the TV to babysit and entertain. No matter how educational the show, television equals inactivity.

If at all possible, choose a licensed child care facility. Licensed facilities are regularly inspected by government agencies. They may cost more, but you may be able to claim the cost for an income tax credit.

Try to find a facility that is close to your job. Some office buildings now offer child care facilities. You'll have the advantage of being able to see your child during the day, and driving to and from work with your child will give you extra time to spend together. If your schedule is flexible, you may even be able to find low-cost or free child care by agreeing to work at a day care center one or more days per week. Besides saving money, you and your child will enjoy sharing the same environment at least part of the week.

Drop your child off early and chat with the caregiver for a few minutes. Ask: "What do you have planned for the children today?" When you pick up your youngster, ask: "What activities did you do today that I can ask Joe about?" I know the time before and after work is precious, but so is your child. Remember, children need to know you care about them. Taking a few minutes when you drop off your child and another few minutes when you pick him up sends the message that you care. Your child may be out of your sight but not out of your mind and heart.

If the caregiver is too busy or not interested in talking to you, consider changing. Caregivers must be able to listen and care one-on-one. That's why the low ratio of children to adults is so important.

When you drop your child off at day care, mention something that relates to the day ahead. Be sure to choose age-related comments. For instance: "Pay very close attention to the book Ms. _____ reads today. You can tell me the story at dinner tonight." Then remember to ask, even if you have to write it down so you don't forget.

Plan to spend an hour or two each week sharing your child's experience in the care facility. Knowing, in detail, about how and where your child spends the day, will enable you to engage him in more meaningful conversation at home. When he talks about a book, you'll know the story. When he tells you about his friends, you'll know who they are. An hour or two per week is not so much. Five to ten minutes each morning and evening will do it.

Drop-off time sets the tone for the day. Rushing around without paying direct attention to your child will hurt his feelings. If you spend ten special minutes with him in the morning, have breakfast together, then spend an additional few minutes saying goodbye before you leave for work, you've already had quality time. Your child won't feel abandoned.

CHORES AND RESPONSIBILITY

It takes a lot of work to raise a family and keep a household going. There are always enough chores for everyone. Doing meaningful chores makes everyone feel like a member of the family. Even the youngest children can do chores. Self-esteem goes up when children know their help is important to the family. Each person can contribute what he is capable of doing.

To a child there is no difference between work and play. If you make working fun, your child will want to do it also. That's why there are play lawnmowers, wheelbarrows, brooms, and vacuum cleaners.

Between the ages of 6 and 11, kids acquire the basic skills they'll need for a lifetime. You hold them back if you do too much for them. Don't "kill" your kids with kindness by doing all their chores for them. But don't overload them with more than their fair share either.

Keep the chores appropriate to the child's age and ability level. I have young female students, third- and fourth-graders, whose families demand they be the homemakers. They prepare dinner, clean the house, put younger siblings to bed, and pick up after their brothers. It is no wonder that they seldom have time or energy left for their studies, and their grades show it. They grow to resent their parents and their siblings. They note every discrepancy between what they are assigned and what the other kids in the house are doing. They are embarrassed in front of their friends and begin to make excuses not to go to school. The downward spiral continues. When a child, at any age, is expected to take on the responsibilities of an adult, everyone ultimately loses.

On the other hand, I also have students who never do anything to help their families. They don't wash dishes, pick up after themselves, or get good grades. These parents mean well; they want their children's lives to be easier than their own. But it doesn't always work that way. Many children who have no responsibilities at home refuse to accept any at school. Most days, there is plenty of time for a child to balance school responsibilities with home chores, and still have time to play.

Finally, don't offer bribes to your children. Family members do things for one another because there are tasks that need to be done. Help your child appreciate the intrinsic rewards: "We all do chores because we're a family. We help one another," or "When we're done with the chores, we'll have more time to spend together."

What kind of chores are appropriate for my child?

Toddlers can:

> *Pick up their toys*
>
> *Put dirty clothes in the laundry pile*
>
> *Put groceries away on the bottom shelves*

Preschoolers can do all the things toddlers can do plus:

> *Set and clear the table (avoid breakables and heavy items)*
>
> *Stack the newspapers*
>
> *Work in the garden*
>
> *Help wash the car*
>
> *Help bake cookies*

Kindergartners can do all of the above plus:

> *Take out the trash*
>
> *Clean their rooms*
>
> *Make their beds (so what if it's not perfect?)*
>
> *Lay out their school clothes*

Elementary school-aged children can do all of the above plus:

Help you prepare dinner

Wash the dishes (be prepared to have some breakage)

Fold the laundry and put it away

WORKING AND PLAYING WITH OTHERS

School is a social environment. Children who know how to interact well with each other will learn more easily in a classroom. There are many ways to help your child learn how to behave well in group settings.

Games naturally require children to work in groups. Prepare your child for the kind of interaction he will encounter at school by playing games at home—anything from Chutes and Ladders™ to Nintendo™, from catch to t-ball. Invite siblings, friends, or neighbors to play. Praise children for taking turns. Don't be surprised if they prefer to make up their own rules, or if rules change along the way. Changing the existing rules to suit the moment is fine. Their agenda is not the same as yours, nor should it be. Just because a game has rules, or because you played it that way, doesn't mean they have to.

Encourage your child to join in group play and to figure out how to be fair. Say: "How will you decide who goes first?" This is a tough question. Give your child time to think about it before answering, and be ready for him to change his mind a few times.

"What are the rules you're going to use? Can you tell them to me?" Another tough question. You might make some suggestions, but don't rush it. Children need to allow their imaginations to wander.

"How will you know when someone wins?" They may not care about winning, or may change the game long before there is a winner.

Should a problem arise, help your child work it out. Don't rush in to solve it for him and his playmates. You can ask: "Can you tell me what the problem is?" When he answers, restate for clarity: "So, you think the problem is _____ (repeat what the child says)." Use the child's words as much as possible. Once you are clear, ask the other child to explain how she sees the problem: "Now it's _____'s turn to tell me what the problem is." Again, restate the child's words. Ask: "Mark thinks this, Marjorie thinks differently. How can we solve the problem between you?" Give each child a turn to respond. Restate what they say. Ask: "How is your solution different from _____'s solution?" Then: "How can we resolve this difference?"

At first, it's tempting to solve the problem yourself, to take the game or other object of contention away, or to separate the kids. While that may cut the noise immediately, and in a few cases may be the best solution, it's not helpful in the long run. You want your child to learn how to resolve disputes without resorting to name-calling and fists.

In such a situation, a good example, as always, can work wonders. When you and your partner have an argument your child witnesses, let him see you solve it by listening to each other and working out a compromise solution. This will be his best example.

Finally, remind your child that no one likes a bully. It is not a way to build real friendships and it will not help in the classroom. Emphasize to your child that he will get along best with his classmates and teacher if he treats them fairly. A teacher may sometimes give in to the child who is the most boisterous just to end a bad situation, but he will resent having to do so. It is in your child's best interest that the teacher enjoy his presence in the classroom. The well-mannered child will receive more positive responses from the teacher and will most likely show greater progress and have positive experiences in school. A strong bond between child and teacher will help your child on his road to success.

Learning to interact, take turns, and work well with a team, like everything else, begins at home. With consistent help, your child will begin to understand these concepts from early on.

TOYS AND PLAYTIME Unstructured playtime is critical to your child's mental and physical development. It balances out the more structured time dedicated to piano practice, gymnastics, acting auditions, chores, and so on. Unstructured time gives your child a chance to use his imagination, to

44

explore, and to find ways to entertain himself. While running around and playing helps build a strong, confident body, inventing toys and games is a precursor for storytelling, reading, and writing. Children who develop their imaginations, who aren't handed the TV remote every time they say they are bored, are hungry learners who will soon devour everything school has to offer. For this reason, I often welcomed my own children's noisy exchanges, the give and take, and the negotiating of unstructured play.

There are many things you can do to encourage creative playtime. Here are some quick, easy tips:

- ◆ Don't buy too many toys. A few well-chosen items are all your child needs. Toys that require the child to invent and imagine have more value than those which only need turning or winding up. Blocks, a couple of beloved stuffed animals, a doll or two, trains, cars, crayons and lots of paper, will go a long way toward preparing your child to use his imagination, to see things in an unconventional way.

- ◆ Make your own toys. Milk cartons, rinsed and drained, make wonderful building blocks for the very young child. Later, with a little bit of glued-on construction paper, they become houses and toy trains. Coffee cans make great containers for small toys and they're easy for your child to carry. An empty oatmeal canister makes a great drum, and it's not too loud.

- ◆ Keep paper, glue, boxes, crayons, safety scissors, and clay on hand. These materials demand creativity. Rule of thumb: allow your child to use them in any way he wishes. As long as what he wants to do is safe, let his imagination fly. Being inventive will teach your child that he doesn't ever have to be bored.

Chapter 2

ORGANIZATION AND ROUTINES

PERHAPS I CAN best express the importance of organization and routines in a child's life by telling you about one of my ninth-grade students. The class had just completed an assignment when I asked them to pass their work forward for grading. One student, whom I had seen doing the exercise, didn't turn his paper in. When I inquired why, he said he couldn't find it. I wasn't surprised. He is one of those students whose pages are constantly falling out of his binder, who doesn't know how to use dividers to separate subjects, who can't find pencils, loses books, misplaces letters to his parents, and ultimately fails many of his classes. He is completely disorganized and his level of success suffers for it.

While it is true that some children appear to be born with excellent organizational skills, most are not. Children have to learn to be organized. Elementary school teachers will work with your child and help her to organize her classwork, but every teacher will tell you how difficult, maybe impossible, it is to help a child who comes from a very disorganized home.

The kid who can't find her homework, even though she did it the night before, is usually the one who also misplaced her lunch box, doesn't have a pencil, has one sock falling down, and a missing shoelace. Hers is the mother who forgot the parent-teacher conference, who didn't return the permission slip, who didn't follow through on her promises.

Occasionally, the parent is organized but the child is not. Usually, the parent just has not taken the time to teach the child some basic organizational skills. If, by nature, you are not an organized person, you owe it to your child to get organized.

Show me a student notebook or portfolio and I can tell you, with great accuracy, what grades the student is earning. Sloppy school papers usually mean sloppy thinking and low grades.

SAME OLD TIME, SAME OLD PLACE

Children thrive on routine. From birth, children do best if they go to sleep every day at the same time, have their meals at the same time, and have regular playtimes. As difficult as it may be to establish and stick to a baby's routine, it is infinitely easier than having a cranky baby who doesn't know when it's time to eat or sleep. The same holds true when you are preparing your child for school. Routines take care of life's little necessities. They provide the structure and time children need to be happy, creative, and successful.

When I became a teacher, after having spent many years in the business world, it was difficult for me to adjust to the bell schedule. In school, the bell dictates when your day begins, when you change subjects, when you eat, when you play, even when you go to the bathroom. The child who is used to following a schedule or has an established routine adapts much more readily to the rhythm of school.

Once a child begins school, she has a lot more responsibilities. It is very important for her to have a schedule which allows time for all of the things she needs to do in a single day. The key to maintaining the schedule is to organize each part of the day. Carve out time slots for all of the day's activities, including basics like meals, playtime, and homework. Be flexible and make the schedule fit the needs of your child and family. For example, if mornings are extra harried, try to factor in a little extra time for the unexpected snags which usually cause delays.

Every home should have a kitchen timer with a loud ringer and a clock with big numbers on its face. Then it's easy to say, "When the clock says seven-thirty we'll read together," or "When the timer goes off it's time for bed." The timer and clock become the dictators of the schedule and your child is less likely to have a quarrel with you. If the schedule is a problem and your child rebels, write the schedule out and post it in a prominent place (the bedroom door and refrigerator work well). You are helping your child learn that there is a time for everything, and there is time to *do* everything when we are organized.

Here's a sample schedule for the young student. Create a similar schedule that fits your family, and then stick with it:

Rise:	6 a.m.	Free play time:	4–5 p.m.
Dress for school:	6–6:30 a.m.	Homework/reading:	5–6 p.m.
Prepare for school:	6:30–7 a.m.	Dinner:	6–6:30 p.m.
Breakfast:	7 a.m.	Prepare for bed:	6:30–7 p.m.
Go to school:	7:30 a.m.	Watch TV or play:	7–7:30 p.m.
School:	8 a.m.–3 p.m.	Read with parent:	7:30–8 p.m.
Snack:	3:30–4 p.m.	Bedtime:	8 p.m.

BEDTIME Set a time and stick with it. Too many children arrive at school tired and listless because they haven't had enough sleep. You can't learn if you are not well rested. Children should have a fixed bedtime for school nights as well as for non-school nights. If your child goes to bed at eight o'clock, she can get up at six. With sufficient sleep she won't feel tired or rushed in the morning. There will be adequate time for getting dressed, eating breakfast, and arriving at school on time. You might want to have a different bedtime on nights when there is no school the next day, or keep the same schedule seven days a week.

Don't break the routine because there's a party or a special show on television. Save parties for the weekend and, trust me, no child has ever died from missing a television show she's certain everyone else will see. Do make certain that your house or apartment is as quiet as possible at your child's bedtime. Playing soft music on the radio can help block out noises you can't eliminate, and may help your child fall asleep.

SCHOOL CLOTHES

School clothes should be set out the night before. Listen to the weather report so you know what to expect, then put out the appropriate clothes. Sending your child to school in a heavy sweater when it's 80 degrees will make her uncomfortable and miserable. Not being dressed appropriately gets in the way of learning.

Your child doesn't need fancy clothes for school, and she doesn't need a new outfit for every day of the week either. It is important that her school clothes are kept in good repair. Make sure her shoelaces are intact, missing buttons have been replaced, clothes are clean and mended. Both you and your child should know that in the morning there will be no discussions or problems about what to wear.

If your child's school gives you the option of a uniform, take it. Uniforms take the hassle out of deciding what to wear. They eliminate arguments about clothes, are less expensive, and save you lots of time.

A PLACE FOR EVERYTHING

Children who are unorganized frequently tell their teacher, "I forgot it at home," "I left it on the table," "It's in my other jacket," or a hundred other excuses. When the teacher asks for something the child has forgotten, the child feels bad. She feels like she has failed, and she has. Small failures add up to big failures. Good students not only do their homework on time, they remember to bring it to school.

Here's an easy way to help your child get organized about her schoolwork: set a box or crate inside the front door. Several children can share the same box. As soon as homework is completed, notes are signed, and supplies are gathered, have your child pack her backpack and put everything she will need for school the next day in the box. This way, she won't be likely to forget anything important—even after a long weekend or during a morning rush.

If your child is having an especially difficult time remembering to put all of her school things together, you could help her by setting an example. Get your own box for your wallet, keys, purse, etc. Who knows, establishing a routine with your child may help you as well.

If the box idea doesn't work for you, then assign one place in the house or apartment where your child keeps her backpack. Insist that she keep it there. Make sure all assignments are put into the backpack as soon they are completed.

Some of you will say that it's the child's responsibility to remember her homework, and it is. But most kids need extra help. The earlier you help your child to establish a place for her school work, the quicker she will learn to do it herself. When you get frustrated because you are still reminding your third-grader to put her school work by the door, think about the last time you put your keys down and then couldn't find them. Remember, our goal is to help our kids be successful in school. Whatever you have to do to help, especially during these early years, do gladly. The payoff will be well worth your effort.

LONG- AND SHORT-TERM PROJECTS

When your child first begins school, her activities will usually be limited to projects she can complete in a short period of time (about an hour or less). As she advances to higher grades she'll be assigned books to read, projects to develop, and reports to compile. These assignments will last for several days or weeks at a time. Some students will begin working the day an assignment is given. Most will procrastinate. After all, Friday seems so far away; two weeks to finish a project seems like forever.

Assisting your child with a long-term project is a very important task. Teachers assign them for multiple reasons. Long-term projects have more depth, demonstrate a student's critical thinking skills, and require planning. Helping your student to budget her time, think ahead, imagine what might go wrong, and plan a backup accordingly will prepare her to complete her work successfully.

When your child receives a long-term project, immediately sit down together and plan how the work will be done. Get a calendar. Mark the due date. Figure out how much work needs to be done on a daily basis. Make plans to get the books and supplies she'll need. Check her progress regularly. Do everything you can to help her complete her work on time. When the project is finally delivered to school, she'll feel terrific about having met the due date.

Most of your child's classmates will be rushing around, trying to complete the assignment the night before it's due. Their work will show it. Or their parents may take over the project instead. The results may be wonderful, but if it's not the child's work, she loses.

In order to be able to plan projects with your child, it is necessary that you talk about school on a regular basis. Develop a routine together. Have your child show you her school work daily. Look at her books, ask her questions. Unless that routine is in place, you won't know about her upcoming projects until she's running around in a panic the night before they're due.

Part II:

The Basics

Chapter 3

READING

WE ARE LIVING in an age in which information reigns supreme. Those who have the information will have the power. Most jobs, including all so-called white collar jobs and many blue collar jobs, involve reading as a major component. It's almost impossible to find any kind of job, anywhere, that doesn't require good reading skills. Also, more and more of our work opportunities will include some use of the Internet, which primarily involves increasing numbers of words appearing on the computer screen. As technology continues to develop and the work force continues to evolve, the importance of reading will also continue to skyrocket.

In order to be a successful adult, it is crucial that your child learn to read with comprehension from a variety of sources (books, magazines, newspapers, the computer screen, and so on), and be able to make connections among everything he's read. You can help your child become a lifelong reader and seeker of information by passing along to him the value you place on reading.

It's difficult, although not impossible, to instill a love of reading in your child if you are not a reader. If you feel unsure of your own reading ability, or if your spouse or another key adult in your child's life cannot read, take heart. Many communities offer free literacy programs and classes. Many schools in larger cities now have parenting centers where adults can learn right along with their children. It's never too late to learn. Most people who claim they hate to read have reading disabilities which they can learn to overcome.

Reading together is a wonderful, inexpensive way to share experiences with your child. It is also the key to problem-solving, learning, and succeeding in school. Early readers start ahead and generally stay ahead. Those whose parents and elder siblings are bookworms tend to learn to read first and best. If you create an environment where reading is valued, the benefits for your child will last a lifetime.

GETTING READY TO READ You're not expected to deliver your child to kindergarten already able to read. You can, however, prepare your child to be *ready* to read by the time he enters school. For children to be successful readers they must, first of all, see well, hear well, be fed and sheltered, and be emotionally healthy. Those are your first responsibilities. Your child's teachers will take over the mechanics of reading, but there is much you can do to help.

Begin reading aloud to your child when he is an infant. Just the sounds of the words prepare your child to begin understanding language skills. When the child is able to sit in your lap with the book in front of you, make connections between the words you're reading and the words on the page. Over time the young child will come to understand that what is on the page is related to what you are saying.

Young children love to hear the same stories over and over. After a while they look at the book and pretend to read to you. Even before they know the words on the page, kids pretend to read. My daughter memorized her favorite stories and delighted in "reading" them to me, including knowing when to turn the page, long before she could truly read the words. Reading is exciting; it leads to a sense of independence, of growing up. Pretend reading indicates the child is connecting the printed word with meaning. This is an essential step in getting your child ready to read.

The child who enters kindergarten never having made a connection between printed words and meaning is at a distinct disadvantage. Knowing that letters on a page have real-world meanings is an advantage you can give your children before they begin school.

Introduce the ABC's and their associated sounds when your child seems ready. "This is a 'B'. It sounds like 'buh.' Let's make that sound together." When the letter comes up in something you are reading, a story about "bees" for example, point out the connection. Follow your child's lead when it comes to introducing the alphabet and the most common sounds. Don't rush. Don't criticize when the child tries to recall a letter and gets it wrong. You say: "A 'D' does look a lot like a 'B'. Let's look at the two letters side-by-side so we can see the difference." Don't make your child anxious. He'll make a lot of errors before he attains accuracy in recognizing the alphabet.

THE SPOKEN WORD

Language is the heart of reading. Readers come from environments rich in spoken language (any language) and filled with printed words (books, magazines, newspapers, greeting cards, signs, and so on) that are frequently read aloud.

Adults, through language, open the door to the world. Adults explain their world to their children as they have experienced it and continue to experience it. Children convert adult talk to what they can understand.

Tell stories to your children about your life, about experiences you've had or plan to have. Narrative stories have beginnings, middles, and ends. Learning to sequence, and to understand sequencing, is part of preparing your child to read. Encourage your child to tell stories as well.

Children want in. They want to understand the why and the how of everything around them. The child whose parents respond in monosyllables, or not at all, soon learns to stop asking questions. Encourage questions. When you don't know the answer, admit it, then try to find out. Your library or bookstore will have many wonderful books to help answer some of the trickiest questions children ask. A series titled *Tell Me Why* is among the best.

READING ALOUD

Everyone, adults and children alike, loves to be read to, especially if the reader reads with expression. Reading to your child regularly, maybe 30 minutes a day, is one of the best things you can do to foster a love for reading. Being read to is great preparation for learning how to read, and it ranks high as quality time for you and your child.

Choose stories your child will enjoy and, if possible, read the material over ahead of time so you don't stumble. Explain difficult words. Make different voices, if you're able, for the different characters in the story. Make sounds that

relate to what you are reading: a dog barking, a giant's foot-steps, a baby crying or laughing. Can't make voices? Try putting on different hats to match the characters. Still feel silly? Take a look at your child's face when you read with expression. His obvious enjoyment at having the story brought to life may ease your initial discomfort. Soon you'll enjoy it as much as he does.

While you're reading, sit side by side or with your child in your lap, so you can look at the words and pictures together. Check for evidence that your child is listening by asking questions about the text. Questions require your child to think about what you are reading.

Ask your child to recall the sequence of events as you're reading. "Do you remember what happened to Peter Rabbit first? What happened to him after that?" Ask him to predict: "What do you think will happen next?" "Why do you think Peter will get home safely?" Allow your child time to think and respond. Talking about what you're reading gets children involved with understanding what the printed words on the page mean.

Don't get tense over whether or not you are using the "right" techniques. Parents naturally use a variety of strategies when reading and eliciting responses from children. Your child will learn just by being exposed to reading. For instance, knowing that the sentences go from the left side of the page to the right, and from the top to the bottom, happens if you occasionally follow along with your finger, or help your child to follow along.

Sharing a beloved book with your child can be the highlight of your day, an intimate moment which will add not only to your child's reading readiness and future success, but to his sense of being loved by you. Set aside time for reading with your child. Disconnect the phone; turn off the television. This time spent one-on-one, without interruption, can have the power to transform you both.

REAL-WORLD READING

You don't always have to stop everything you're doing to read with your children. Since we learn by connecting what we don't know to what we already know, you can use real reading experiences which naturally occur throughout the day to supplement set-aside reading time. For example: when cooking, read the recipe directions out loud. When driving, read the road signs. Children need to learn that print and speech are related.

Don't overdo it. Don't point out every sign every time you leave the house. Children also need time to observe and to think. Do read something aloud if your child asks, "What does that say?" Those are learning moments of great importance. Those moments show that your child is making connections between the letters he sees and the meaning they have.

The real world provides us with an abundance of reading materials: the Sunday comics, lists of chores, mail, shopping lists, instructions for all sorts of things, labels on cans and bottles, street signs, grocery bags, advertisements, cereal boxes, and, of course, the daily newspaper. All provide lots of opportunity for discussion. Relate what is in the text to personal experiences. For example, while pointing to an advertisement in the newspaper, explain: "This ad says 'Buy a new car today.'" Then say, "Remember when we went shopping for our car. We knew where to go because we looked in the newspaper. We read the addresses to see where the car stores are, and found out how much the car costs by looking at the prices. Then we shopped for the car." Or "We're planning to buy a new car someday. Reading the advertisements will help us to know where to go to buy it."

Make a grocery list from the food section of the paper. Connect the words to what children like to eat. "This word says 'bread.' We need to buy some bread today so let's write down the word 'bread.'" Try labeling items around the house to help your children make connections between things and words. Together you can also create books with pictures cut from magazines and newspapers. Label the pictures clearly. Seeing a word next to what it represents is a great visual tool for your child. Plus, your child will return over and over again to books you made together.

SELECTING BOOKS

Story books are good for sequence, prediction, and a variety of vocabulary words. Young children love to hear the same stories over and over. Share some of the books you loved as a child with your children.

Every child should have a library card as soon as he is old enough. Libraries and librarians are wonderful resources. Ask them for suggestions for age-appropriate books. Make trips to the library an adventure. Explore the thousands of books available for free. Devote a canvas bag specifically for borrowing books from the library. It's also a good way to keep track of borrowed books.

Buy books. It's never too early to start a home library for your child. Bookstores, library sales, thrift shops, garage sales, gifts, or trading with peers are all wonderful ways to acquire a home library. Owning a book you can return to time and again is like having a friend on call. Owning a book helps to teach children to take care of their things.

Some stories have no pictures. Encourage your child to visualize for himself. You might say: "This story is about the three little pigs. Let's find a picture of a pig," or "Do you remember what a pig looks like from when we visited the children's petting zoo?" or "They live in a house built of straw. What would a house of straw look like?" Encourage your child to describe, to make his own pictures to fit the text. Older children might illustrate a text on their own.

Read other books that are natural offshoots of the first one. For example, if you're reading about Peter Rabbit going into Mr. McGregor's garden, a good choice for another reading session might be a book about gardens and growing vegetables.

When choosing books, select themes related to children. They are the center of their universe. They connect with things that relate to them personally. For example, an airplane travel book may be wonderful for a child who has traveled by plane or who is about to go on an airplane trip, but may not appeal to a child who has never seen an airplane.

Add books on social issues as the child develops. There are children's books about recycling, giving to charity, caring for elderly family members, saving animals, and practically anything else you may be interested in. It's never too early to begin teaching your child the values you hold important.

Books are also available to help children through tough or challenging times. A birth or death, a hospital visit, the loss of a pet, or moving to a new house can be more easily understood by a child if he reads about it. Librarians and children's bookstore personnel are excellent resources to help you with your selections.

When your child is able to read by himself, help him select books he can read to you. Children's books are no longer nonsensical, whimsical pieces of fluff. They teach, inspire, excite, comfort, and challenge. Share these experiences with your child by reading together regularly.

As your child grows and develops, what he reads or hears read should also change. Here are some general guidelines to help you choose appropriate reading material:

♦ Nursery rhymes are perfect for the infant. At about three months a child will begin to anticipate a rhyme's ending. Rhyme is predictable and structured. The repetitions become comfortable. Rhymes help children learn to listen, which is an important part of the reading process.

♦ Two-year-olds enjoy simple pictures and repeated words and phrases. That's why Dr. Seuss books are so popular, even with the youngest children.

♦ Three-year-olds like books with rhymes, repeated ideas, and themes. Books about seasons and holidays, people at work, and pictures of families doing things you do are popular.

- Four-year-olds like stories which have some drama and humor, a well-crafted plot and action. These stories should have a beginning, middle, and end.

- Five-years-olds are ready for fairy tales, longer, more elaborate stories, and poetry. They may even be able to read some of the simplest books to you.

- Six-year-olds enjoy books which motivate them to do things, special-interest books about holidays, ethnic groups, traditions, or books relating to family issues like divorce, death, or visits to the doctor.

READING IN SCHOOL   If your child goes to school already able to make the connection between spoken words, ideas, and writing, he will be ready for reading. There is a sequence agreed to by most educators for learning to read. The child who is ready to read moves through the sequence quickly and by the end of the first grade is already reading simple sentences.

On the other hand, some students, especially those whose home environments are not rich in language, are still trying to read simple sentences as late as third grade. Don't be alarmed if your child is not perfectly aligned with the guide that follows. Some students start off a little slower, but quickly catch up to their peers. The following is offered as a basic guide, not as absolute rules which must be followed. On the other hand, if you are concerned about your child's progress, do contact the teacher and ask for a reading conference. You may spot a problem that the teacher, with twenty or thirty-plus students in his classroom, might have missed.

In general:

Kindergartners and first-graders are learning to:

identify all the letters in the alphabet

know long and short vowel sounds

know the consonant sounds

extract meaning from written text (decoding)

read simple sentences

Second-graders are learning:

syntax (sentence structure) and grammar

how to read for main idea

how to predict

sequence (what comes first, second, etc.)

the difference between fiction and nonfiction

simple declarative sentences and questions

Third-graders are learning:

to identify the main idea

how to predict

to recognize supporting details (Jose is a good student because he reads every day, does all his homework, etc.)

cause and effect (If Mary studies, she will do well on the exam. If the bee drinks the flower's pollen, then the bee will make honey.)

topic sentences (the main idea of a paragraph)

Current emphasis is on beginning to read in pre-kindergarten and/or kindergarten. But no matter when they start, children should be reading with fluency and understanding by the end of third grade.

Once your child is in school the teacher is the primary source of reading instruction, but that doesn't mean you should stop reading at home. Quite the opposite. Parents should continue reading daily with their children. Instead of the parent doing all of the reading, the child will be sharing the reading activity by doing some of the reading on his own. Children can read to parents and discuss what they are reading in school.

Enforce a convenient period of time each day (at least 15 minutes) for your child to read silently a text of his choice. Comic books, newspapers, novels, biographies, almost anything that interests him can be appropriate reading material. Check for comprehension by asking him to tell you about what he's read. If you notice that your child can read the words, but doesn't appear to understand what they mean in a paragraph, consult with his teacher. Some students learn to decode individual words but need more help in getting meaning from the story.

Stay involved. There is a direct correlation between parents who are involved in and supportive of their children's education and children who are successful.

READING IDEAS It's important not to lose sight of the fact that reading is fun. You want your child to enjoy reading, not feel it is about pleasing you.

Here are some easy and entertaining projects, games, and activites your kids will like:

- ◆ Cut letters out of old sponges or pieces of styrofoam, or purchase a set, to play with in the bathtub.

- ◆ Attend story hour at the library or in your favorite bookstore, or invite relatives to prepare a story to read to the rest of the family. The stories don't have to be children's stories. When the reader is animated the children will enjoy the rhythm of the story even if they don't always understand it. However, do use common sense in making selections.

◆ Hop to the alphabet. The children listen for and hop to the letters of the alphabet as you call them out. Mix the letters with numbers or words. You say "D," the child hops. Call out "dog," the child stands still. Don't scold when your child hops for "dog." Remember, it's a game. The primary goal is to have fun while learning to recognize the sounds of the alphabet.

◆ Label items in the house. Print legibly. Hang the words on the things themselves. Start with things that can be easily labeled and have simple names like "door," "lamp," "table," "book."

◆ Turn family picture albums into books by creating captions. Read the captions to your child. You might even want to make stories centering around family events, with words and pictures combined.

◆ Things that happen to the family make wonderful books. For example: The Day Uncle Joe Came to Visit. Illustrate with photos, pictures from magazines, and children's own illustrations.

◆ Create your own books using stickers or newspaper and magazine clippings pasted onto a few pages attached with staples, sewing yarn, or other fasteners. You and your child might create a picture book of things that begin with 'A' (apple, apricot, ant, artichoke, Aunt Mildred) or collections of things that go together (animals found at home, in the zoo, fruit and vegetables we find in the supermarket or in the refrigerator, clothing in our closets or drawers, foods I like to eat).

◆ Start a reading circle. Each day a different person in the family, from the youngest child to live-in grandparents, brings something to read to the reading circle. The choice is entirely up to the person whose turn it is. You might read the stock report one night, a recipe another, and a book about cats the third.

◆ Join or start a reading book club. Invite the neighborhood children over for cookies and punch. Each child is to bring a book to share with the group. If they are able, they can read the book. If not, they can just tell the story, show the pictures, or carry it around saying, "It's mine." The emphasis is on sharing reading experiences. One of the best ways to get children excited about reading is to have other children share their excitement and their favorite stories.

◆ Play a variation of the game "May I?" Children identify letters you hold up on index cards. They advance for each letter they identify. Those who reach home base get a treat/prize. Allow everyone to be a winner.

◆ Post a list of new words on a long sheet of paper and hang it on a wall or by a door. Add words as your child learns them or wants to learn them. Select words your child asks about while reading a book, seeing a street sign, or just listening to a conversation. Watching the list grow will make your child feel proud of his progress, and it will remind him of what each new word means.

Chapter 4

WRITING

AS THE twenty-first century approaches, writing is becoming an extremely important skill. Electronic communication may reduce the need for good handwriting, but the need to communicate our ideas precisely to people we may know only through a computer network will escalate. Without the help of facial expression, hand movements, and body language, written communication depends on clear thinking, precise expression, and exact word choice. Getting your young child comfortable with using and interpreting the written word will have long-term benefits. Students who are able to express their ideas clearly in writing have a much better chance of doing well in school and in their adult lives.

GETTING READY TO WRITE

Writing is the fourth learning step in language, and the most complex. Children learn first by hearing language, then by speaking, third by reading, and fourth by writing. But just because writing is highest in the language chain, that doesn't mean we should wait until the first three steps are mastered before beginning. Once toddler stage has been reached the child is ready to begin writing.

The physical act of writing begins with exercising fine motor skills: building blocks, manipulating Play-doh™, separating one noodle or pea from the rest of the dinner. The fifteen-month-old who prefers to feed herself (with her fingers, of course) is practicing the skills she'll need for holding a pencil. When she zeros in on the one piece of diced peach she wants, she's getting ready to dot her i's and cross her t's.

Developing hand-eye coordination through play is a pre-writing step. Spring clothespins, available at hardware and craft shops, can become wonderful toys to help your child develop her manual dexterity. Show your preschooler how to press on the clothespin and pick up small objects with the open end (straws, colored rods, and thin hair rollers are great). At first, she'll have a good deal of trouble holding the clothespin open, but as she practices over the months she'll become quite adept at picking things up with it.

Clay and Play-doh™ are also great for fostering manual dexterity and self-expression. Kids love to shape the soft, malleable material. Your child's early creations won't look like anything, but they don't have to. The squeezing, rolling, pounding, and pulling actions used to work the clay strengthen her fingers and hands and prepare her for the fine act of writing.

Finger painting is a mess, but what a fun way to get ready for writing. From smearing paint with the whole hand, to making precise lines with the tip of one finger, your child is developing the skills she'll need.

Crayons are also an important pre-writing tool. Using crayons allows a child to explore written or drawn forms, connect ideas with images, and gain control of her fingers and hands. A child holds a crayon as she will later hold a pencil or pen. Learning to direct the crayon to where she wants the color is an important fine motor skill that needs a great deal of practice. She'll begin by rubbing the crayon randomly, or so it will seem. Those haphazard marks are actually the child's attempt to control her design. She's making connections between what she's doing, how she's moving her hands and fingers, and what is happening on the paper. Watch a child during her early coloring experiences. The concentration is as intense as a scientist pouring the final drop of a potent chemical into a glass beaker.

You can insist that your preschooler color on paper only, but some crayon marks on the walls and furniture are inevitable. A young child doesn't have full mastery of her strokes, and she may get carried away from time to time. Crayon marks on the wall are also a testing of her limits, and yours. Don't make her so afraid of going off the paper that she stops trying. Inexpensive butcher paper, sheets of newsprint, or used grocery

bags opened and turned inside-out can provide large, clean writing surfaces. Tape the paper to the wall and instruct your child that writing on the walls is not okay, but writing on the paper is fine.

When your child creates a "work of art," write her name in large letters on the paper. Tell her you are spelling her name. Around the age of three she will begin to want to write her own name on her artwork, and on everything else that belongs to her. Don't expect her early attempts at writing to be legible. Within a year, her letters will become recognizable, although they may not be consistent or perfect. The physical act of writing requires the fine motor coordination your child doesn't yet have. What you're seeing is the process of learning to write unfold.

Writing is a mental as well as a physical skill. The mental act of writing begins as soon as your child tells you a story: "Today I went to the park." "Brother hit me." "My doll wants to eat lunch with me." While your child can work on her physical skills without much intervention on your part, the mental act of writing requires your involvement.

You don't have to wait until your child can write the alphabet with a ball-point pen before you help her to "write" her first story. Take a piece of her artwork and ask her to tell you about the picture. Your child may be confused, or she may answer with one word: "ball." Take it from there: "Is this a ball?" Explain that you are going to write down the words she says. Write slowly and deliberately. Read her words back to her. "This is what you told me about your picture. I am writing it down so later we can read about your picture." Keep it simple: "The boy has a garden." "This is a dog." "I'm happy." Later in the day return to the labeled picture. Read aloud the words the child "wrote." She may want to add something, or she may not.

Dictating her ideas to you is your child's first step in connecting the mental process to the physical process. You may feel like you're doing all the work, but the creating is hers. Encourage her to tell you stories that you can write down. As she gets older she can illustrate her stories. Or she can draw pictures first, then create stories to match.

Although you are not expected to deliver your child to kindergarten already writing essays, early reading and writing preparation will positively affect her educational progress and success. Preschool classes, head-start enrichment programs, and language-rich day care programs can help prepare your child. But don't worry if she can't attend an organized program. With your help she can still be ready.

If your child has had the opportunity to develop her hand-eye coordination, has practiced her fine motor skills, worked with crayons, written her name, and understands that the words on a page mean something, then she is ready for school. If she knows the letters of the alphabet and can recognize some words—remember the pictures you've been labeling for her and hanging all over the house for the past two years—she's ready to learn to read and write.

Children who begin kindergarten without any pre-reading or pre-writing skills are already behind. Because many schools still "track" students from the earliest grades, a less prepared student may be classified, however wrongly, as a "slow" learner—a label which could follow her throughout her school career.

If your child has not mastered some simple skills, and/or if she appears less mature than her age group, you may want to consider holding her back a year. There is no natural law which decrees all children are ready for school at precisely the same moment. Your child is ready for school when she's ready.

HELPING YOUR CHILD ONCE SCHOOL STARTS Teaching your child to write is part of the school's responsibility, but your role does not end when she enters the classroom. Remain involved, work with her at home, and know what's going on at school. Make sure you are available to help her with her assignments and to check over her work.

Here's a general idea of writing development in the classroom:

Kindergartners are learning:

the alphabet

to write their name

the days of the week

First-graders are beginning to work with:

simple sentences

spelling

dictating stories or ideas to the teacher

Second-graders are:

stringing sentences together

writing short narratives about themselves

writing short stories they invent

Third-graders are:

writing complex paragraphs

grouping ideas together

writing in response to things they are reading

Aside from your child's school and homework, create opportunities for her to write. The young child can dictate a story that you write down. Leave spaces for her to add the words she can write. Or have her include herself in the story by filling in her name wherever it's called for. Stories will get more complicated as she reads more and as her writing skills increase. When she is ready, she can write her own stories and then read them to you.

Writing letters is another way to develop your child's writing skills. Not only is it a wonderful way to stay in touch with friends and relatives, but kids, like all of us, love to receive mail. A child can send a picture to grandma, write letters to cousins or pen pals, or send away for free samples from companies. Once she's established herself as a letter-writer, her growth will be phenomenal. She'll come to you with her own ideas for writing, and her skills will improve tremendously.

Chapter 5

MATH

THE MERE THOUGHT of math sends some parents, myself included, into a panic. Recollections of confusing algebraic equations, geometric formulas, and logarithm tables have convinced us that we are incapable of helping our children learn. But during the early years, your child is learning the foundation for higher mathematics. It is extremely important that you help him to understand basic concepts and feel comfortable manipulating numbers. Although this may sound a little scary, relax. Even the most "mathematically challenged" adult knows enough math to help a young child get ready for school.

**GETTING READY
TO DO MATH** Just as with reading, children begin learning math as infants. Silly games and songs are often a child's first introduction to ordinal numbers (numbers that denote order; i.e., first, second, third . . .): "One potato, two potato, three potato, four," or "One little piggy goes to market, the second little piggy stays home. . ."

Mathematical relationships are all around us. You can begin to familiarize your child with basics such as size and shape by explaining, "This is a ball. This is a bigger ball."

"Look at the peas, they are smaller than the carrots. They are round like your ball. This carrot slice is like a circle or a donut."

Young children love to count. It gives them a sense of control over their environment. Opportunities to count are all around. "How many fingers does baby have?" Touch each finger as you count them: "One, two, three, four, five. Baby has five fingers on his hand." You can count up to ten after the child has mastered five. Count often. When feeding the baby, count mouthfuls: "One mouthful, two, three. . . ," and so on. Don't overdo it. You can quit counting after five, even if the child is still eating. Count at the market: "We're buying one banana, two bananas, three bananas." Or count at the playground: "There are one, two, three children on the swings." Counting can even make chores fun: "Let's count how many blocks you can put away."

At first, keep the numbers small. The goal is for your child to connect numbers with meaning. There's no need to count past ten until your child, at about age four, indicates an interest in counting more items. By then he'll be counting his blocks, his action figures, and the place settings on the dining table.

Addition is a natural progression from counting and can be introduced similarly: "If we have one hand here, and one hand here, then we have two hands. One plus one is two." Just as with counting, keep the numbers small. Add like objects. Although you understand that one apple and one orange equals two pieces of fruit, to a young child they remain one apple and one orange. It is best to add one apple to another apple, and one orange to another orange. The goal is for your child to understand the concept of putting two or more things together.

Just as adding proceeds from counting, subtraction is an extension of addition. Again, it is best to illustrate the concept to your child with real objects: "If I have three ice creams—count them: one, two, three—and you eat one, then we have two ice creams left." Let your child eat the ice cream and then count what's left over.

Set theory may sound complicated, but your child practices it every time he sorts his socks by color, separates his blocks by size, or isolates the peas on his plate from the carrots. Set theory simply involves separating a group into sets based on some kind of relationship. Encourage your child to notice the differences and similarities between objects in order to get him more comfortable with set theory.

As an added resource, books can help reinforce basic mathematical concepts for your child. Dr. Seuss's early childhood books do a splendid job of integrating fun and learning. *One Fish, Two Fish* (Random House, 1960) is a good one. Visit your local bookstore or library for hundreds of other options.

HELPING YOUR CHILD ONCE SCHOOL STARTS

If your child has a handle on counting to ten, adding very simple numbers, and perhaps also subtracting a few numbers by the time he's old enough for kindergarten, you've done a terrific job of getting him ready for school. Some educators fear that if a child enters kindergarten already knowing his numbers, he'll be bored. Don't worry; school will reinforce concepts he already knows. He will quickly move on to count bigger numbers, to play with the numbers he's already learned, and to write numbers. A good kindergarten classroom is a rich environment offering many opportunities for learning.

Once your child begins school, your job is to reinforce the concepts his teacher introduces. Check his classwork on a daily basis and set aside time to help him with his homework. Examine the worksheets your child brings home. Ask him to explain them to you. By listening carefully while your child teaches you the same concepts he is learning in the classroom, you are reinforcing his learning. This is also a great way to identify any problems he may be having.

For additional reinforcement, create worksheets to complete with your child. It's not enough to hand your child an assignment and expect him to learn by himself. Although he will undoubtedly learn something, his understanding of math concepts will be stronger when you take the time to teach him. Talking through math assignments is also preparation for the more complex word problems he will encounter in later grades.

The ease with which your child understands and is able to manipulate numbers in the early grades will largely determine how well he'll do in math later on. Your attitude is critical. Statements like, "I don't know much math and I'm doing fine," are a disservice to your child. Likewise, messages, however subtle, such as "girls can't do math" are also discouraging. When your child complains that "this is too hard," that is your signal to help him practice. Respond with, "I know this seems difficult now. Remember when you were learning to count and had trouble remembering seven comes after six? Now you know how to count all the way to one hundred. With lots of practice you'll be able to add all of these numbers. Let's start with two of the numbers first."

Break problems down into smaller parts for your child. Whenever possible, use real-life situations: "Pretend we're at the grocery story. First we buy a can of orange juice for four cents. Write down four. (The child writes 4.) Then we buy a banana for eleven cents. (The child writes 11 under the 4.) How much money have we spent so far?" (The child now adds 4 + 11.) If the child is having difficulty with the concept of adding, use jellybeans (or pieces of cereal, or raisins) to demonstrate. This will help him visualize the abstract: 4 jellybeans + 11 jellybeans can be counted and eaten. Once the concept is understood, the child will be able to add any numbers together.

Reinforce learning. "Remember when you said you couldn't add those numbers? Then you were able to add them by counting the jellybeans. Now you can add numbers together in your head. It's easy for you because you are becoming good at math. As you practice you'll get better and better."

Once your child starts learning the multiplication tables, plan on spending a lot of time helping him memorize them. The student who never masters multiplication has serious difficulty doing more complex mathematical problems. Praise him for being able to recite the multiplication tables first by two's, then three's, then four's, and all the way to nine's.

Here's a basic idea of what your child will learn in school:

Kindergartners are learning:
> *to count*
> *basic addition*

First-graders are learning:
> *ordinal numbers and counting*
> *basic addition and subtraction*
> *set theory*
> *how to measure with a ruler*

Second-graders are learning:
> *to count by two's*
> *measurements*
> *word problems*
> *more complex addition and subtraction*

Third-graders are learning:
> *addition and subtraction*
> *multiplication tables*
> *time concepts*

MATH IDEAS

Besides reviewing home- and classwork with your child, you can help him feel comfortable with numbers by incorporating math concepts into daily activities. Setting the dinner table is an opportunity to review basic math. During the preschool years you'll say, "One spoon for mommy. One spoon for you. How many is one spoon and one spoon?" The first time he says two spoons before you do, praise him. "Look, you know how to add."

Later, table-setting math can become more complex. "How many people are having dinner tonight? How many plates will you need? If we have five people eating dinner, we need five forks. Brother Jimmy is too young to have his own knife. How many knives will we need?" He then subtracts one knife from the total needed. "If there are five people, and we each have one fork, one knife, and one spoon, how many utensils will you need for everyone?" To solve this problem the child employs both multiplication and set theory.

Grocery shopping offers another wonderful opportunity to do math problems. Count how many apples you're buying. Measure how long the cucumbers are. Weigh the grapes on the grocery scales to introduce, or reinforce, what makes a pound.

Complex ideas about volume, weight, and quantity can also be taught at the grocery store. Weight is different than size or quantity. For example: a pound of franks can contain six, eight, or ten hot dogs depending on the size of each. A pound of strawberries contains more pieces than a pound of apples. Only two boxes of cereal fit into a grocery bag, but the same bag can hold four boxes of spaghetti.

Math is all around us. Helping your child to feel comfortable with numbers and to see math problems wherever he looks will play a significant role in his math success.

PART III:

School and Beyond

Chapter 6

SCHOOL DAYS

WHEN THE General Motors plant in Van Nuys, California closed in the late 1980s, hundreds of my high school students were forced to reexamine their future prospects. Their parents had worked for GM for the past 35 years, and they fully expected to continue the family tradition. Since many of their parents had little formal education (few had graduated from high school), many of my students weren't too concerned about their education either. With the plant closing, and the subsequent loss of thousands of high-paying factory jobs, those students who had not taken college prep courses were at a distinct disadvantage.

Each year there are fewer and fewer well-paying jobs available for high school graduates, let alone dropouts. Plenty of opportunities exist, however, for those with higher education or training beyond high school. It is estimated that the latest generation can expect as many as three major career changes in a lifetime. In order to be ready for the challenges of a shifting workplace, the education our children obtain must be of the highest caliber. It is increasingly important that young people take advantage of all the educational opportunities available to them.

Based on experiences with my own youngsters, the children of family and friends, and the thousands I've taught, I firmly believe that the quality of one's education depends on the student and her family more than the institution she attends. Given the same opportunities and choices, some youngsters become actively involved in school, take challenging courses, join after-school activities, enter contests, and apply for scholarships. Others choose to remain on the fringe, mere shadows in the educational process.

The child who volunteers to be class monitor, asks for extra work, and is comfortable walking into the principal's office is frequently the same one who becomes president of the high school senior class or owner of a company. It isn't enough to just attend school every day, although that is certainly a start. Becoming involved and taking ownership of one's education is a prerequisite for success.

Parents set the tone. When you value education and hard work, your child's accomplishments will rise. Without parental reinforcement, schools seldom do a good job of motivating a youngster. The student whose parent stands firmly behind her and who works alongside her begins her education with an advantage that even expensive private schools or small class sizes can't beat.

FED, CLOTHED, AND EQUIPPED You must deliver your child to school knowing she is loved and cared about. If your child believes you love her, she will transfer that sense of acceptance to her teacher. She'll begin by believing the teacher cares about her. Her anxiety about leaving you and going to school will be greatly reduced.

Begin your child's school day with an extra tight hug, an affectionate kiss, some loving and encouraging words: "I'm so proud of you." "I can't wait until you come home and tell me about what you did in school today." "I miss you when you're at school, but I know you're having a good time and you'll have lots to tell me about when you come home."

Feed her. No child can learn if she's concentrating on her next meal. The child who is sitting in school nursing a growling, empty stomach isn't paying attention to the phonics lesson. It is your responsibility to see that your child is fed. No matter what your income level, from wealthy to food stamp recipient, you must provide your child with a nourishing breakfast. If you absolutely cannot, make certain there is a breakfast program at school and see that your child participates.

Likewise, your child must come to school dressed for learning. Clothes don't need to be fancy or even new. They do need to be clean and mended. Children can be very cruel to one another. They quickly focus on those who dress differently, who come to school with torn or dirty clothing, or so dressed up they are afraid to move. Just like hunger, children who are self-conscious about their appearance have a tough time concentrating on the day's lessons. Visit the school. See what students wear and then dress your kid accordingly.

If you can't afford to purchase school clothes or uniforms, call or visit the school and tell them. Every school has a PTA or some other community assistance program. Seek out the help you need and get your child to school appropriately dressed for learning.

Your child should also have the necessary supplies. On or before the first day of school, you will receive a list of required supplies. These may include a backpack, a box to hold pencils and other small objects, a glue stick, scissors, paper, etc. Shopping for school supplies is a major event in a young child's life. It feels very grown-up to have a backpack or briefcase like mom's, or to be getting ready to go off to school just as dad goes off to work. Make the shopping trip special. Don't let your child go to school on the first day without the required supplies. The other students will be comparing what they have to what your child has. You don't need to buy the biggest or the most expensive of anything. Just purchase the items on the list.

As with your child's school clothing or uniforms, if you can't afford school supplies, find out who can help. Schools have funds or know of organizations that offer assistance for these kinds of emergencies. Don't wait until after school begins if the supplies are supposed to be in class the first day. You don't want your child to begin her school career making excuses, hiding, pretending, or lying to her classmates and teacher.

A child who comes to school hungry, dirty, or without the necessary supplies sends a message to the teacher and the administrators. The message is: "My parents don't care about me or my education." This may not be how you feel at all. You may have a dozen reasons for not being able to take care of your child's needs. Yet, even if you have a new baby at home, work long hours, have no money, don't speak English, etc., you are still responsible for delivering your child to school ready to learn each and every day. No matter what arrangements you have to make, see that your child arrives fed, clothed, loved, and with the proper supplies.

ATTENDANCE

When Margo (not her real name) entered my ninth-grade class, she was reading and writing at a third-grade level. I checked her school records and discovered that she had been absent over a hundred days a year since kindergarten. When I added up Margo's total days of attendance, I realized that she was a ninth-grader by age, but only a third-grader in total school attendance. Her medical records did not show any indication of chronic illness. There was no logical reason why she was not attending school regularly.

A conference with Margo's parents revealed the following: during kindergarten, first, second, and third grades, Margo, the eldest child, often stayed at home to help her mother care for her younger brothers and sisters. Fluent in English, Margo also assisted her parents by translating for them with the landlord, the DMV, the unemployment office, and on numerous other occasions.

It was no surprise when Margo, by fourth grade, began to complain of upset stomachs, headaches, and bad dreams. She had a whole list of reasons why she was too ill to attend school, and her parents believed all of them. Being ill was Margo's way of avoiding feeling incompetent and stupid. Margo failed all of her ninth-grade classes, started summer school, then quit, and dropped out of high school at age fifteen.

There are far too many Margos who never get a chance at an education because their parents don't send them to school regularly. Your child belongs in school every day. Daily attendance is one of the basics, just like being fed, clothed, sheltered, and loved.

Usually, when a child reports having a headache, an upset stomach, or another minor ailment that is not accompanied by fever, she is stalling. The message is "I'm not prepared to go to school today," or "There's going to be a test I didn't study for," or "I didn't do the homework," or "There's a kid at school who beats me up and steals my lunch money," or "My teacher frightens me," or "I want to watch TV." And so on.

It's not always easy to know when your child is truly ill and when she's just trying to avoid school. However, if you have daily contact with your child, and regularly discuss schoolwork, relationships, projects, etc. with her, you're more likely to be aware of issues that are troubling her. With your help and guidance, she may be able to work out her problems more easily. The result will be fewer mornings when she reports, "I'm too sick to go to school today."

In the absence of fever, a rash, a cough, or other outwardly observable symptoms, your child is probably well enough to attend school. When she says she's too sick, you say, "I know you're feeling like you are too sick to go to school. Sometimes I think I'm too sick to go to work (or take care of the family), but usually it's because there's something I have to do at work (or at home) that I don't want to do. What's happening at school today?" Then listen. Your child may insist, "No, I really don't feel well." If you're not convinced this is a legitimate illness (e.g., she hasn't thrown up), then take a stand: "I know you would rather stay home today, but I think you will feel better soon and I don't want you to miss a day of school. If you get sick at school, tell your teacher. The school will call me." If the child still hesitates, write down a phone number where you can be reached. Give it to her and say, "If you don't feel better, tell your teacher to call me at this number. I'll come get you right away." Having the added security of knowing that you're there for her may make the difference between attending school or staying at home.

If you decide that your child should stay home, make certain staying home is about getting better. If a child is too sick to attend school, she should not watch television, talk on the phone, or visit with friends. Quiet play, booktime, and lots of naps are much more conducive to recovery.

A child who is too sick to attend school on Friday should continue to rest and take naps throughout the weekend. Don't get into the pattern of having a "sick" child on Friday (lots of teachers give tests on Fridays) who has a miraculous recovery just as the last bus leaves for school, or at the end of the day when the school dismissal bell rings. Once all "danger" of having to attend school has passed, your child may announce she feels well enough to run around and play with her friends for the rest of the weekend. No way! Friday's "sick" child needs to rest all weekend in order to be ready to attend school on Monday. If she's truly sick (sometimes she will be), she'll welcome the quiet time and benefit from the extra rest. On the other hand, there should be no rewards for skipping school.

Will you be wrong sometimes? Of course. You might send your child to school with an upset stomach only to have the nurse call you an hour later because she threw up all over her desk. Trust me, that's rare. Use your better judgment and make sure your child misses as little school as possible.

Routine dental and doctor appointments should be arranged for after-school hours. If more parents insisted on non-emergency appointments in the late afternoon, more dentists and doctors would provide them. If your child's dentist or doctor won't accommodate your request, then find one who will.

Don't schedule family vacations during school time. You might have a wonderful outing, and there is definitely value in having the family together, but it may take weeks after you return for your child to catch up with her classwork. During that time she will be under additional stress, possibly wiping out any benefits from the vacation. Teachers do not have to provide make-up work for children who miss school to take an extended holiday.

Remember that even when your child is home, at the dentist's, or on vacation, her teacher continues to teach, her classmates continue to learn, and she is missing out. It's always a good idea to have the names and phone numbers of several reliable classmates your child can call for missed work. If your child must be absent for longer than two days, call the school and request the work she will be missing. Chances are, even if the child is ill, she is well enough to do some math problems, read the short story her classmates are reading, or write the composition her teacher assigned. When she returns after an illness she'll fit right in if she's completed the missed work. Of course, there will still be some experiences she won't be able to make up. That's the loss for being away from school.

Absence breeds more absence. Students who haven't gotten the missed assignments are often reluctant to return to class. They feel left out. They may have missed an essential part of the lesson which is the basis for the rest of the unit. They would rather continue to stay home.

I can't say it loud enough or often enough: Your child belongs in school every day.

MEDICAL CARE AND EMERGENCY INFORMATION

When you enroll your child in school the health office will require her immunization records, birth certificate, and residence information. In addition, you'll be asked to complete an emergency information card. Emergency information includes the name of your doctor or hospital and the names and phone numbers of people to call in case of an emergency. Please provide an accurate listing of people, including yourself, who can be reached during the day. Keep the information up-to-date. If you change jobs or move, alert the school of your new phone number. Children get very upset if they need their parents but can't reach them. Don't rely on a young child, or even an older one, to remember emergency phone numbers and other pertinent information. Most school emergencies are minor, but on the rare occasion when a serious incident has occurred, the life at risk may be your child's.

Alert the school if your child needs medical attention during the day, takes any medications, has allergies, weak kidneys, is diabetic, or has any other condition which might affect her time in school.

SCHOOL RULES AND BEHAVIOR

A child raised in a home where she is respected and is expected to respect other people and their property, where she is taught early to say "please" and "thank you," and where foul language is not tolerated from anyone, will rarely have a behavior problem in school. On the other hand, if your home environment sounds like an Eddie Murphy cop movie, don't expect your child to behave differently in the classroom.

I once suspended a student for using the "f" word in my classroom. When his parent came in for a conference, the child's language was peppered with "f—ing this" and "f—ing that." He was not corrected once by his parent. While I can't prove a connection between using foul language in school and having poor grades, the fact is that that student did receive four F's and two D's from six different teachers on his first high school report card. He hadn't yet learned that there is a difference between street behavior and school behavior. His use of inappropriate language was symptomatic of his overall lack of self-discipline.

Because the young student in the example above hadn't learned the difference between street talk and school talk, I never did get around to teaching him Shakespeare's sonnets. If your child comes to school knowing how to behave herself, then the teacher can concentrate on helping her learn to read, write, and compute. If she hasn't learned to sit in a seat because you never required it at home, what can her teacher do? It doesn't take more than a few months of poor behavior before a child falls hopelessly behind her classmates. Year after year of poor behavior throws a child's education further and further behind her peers', and may eventually lead to failure or dropping out.

Every teacher establishes rules for her classroom. While most teachers have the same basic rules (no hitting, no throwing, respect other people's property, etc.), there may be some differences. Teacher A may allow children to get up to sharpen their pencils any time while teacher B expects children to raise their hands before leaving their seats. You can help your child adjust by reminding her that at her friend's house there are certain rules (maybe she is allowed lots of TV time) while in your home there are other rules (TV is limited to a half-hour on school nights). School is the same: each classroom has its own rules. Children must learn those rules and respect them.

If the school calls complaining about your child's behavior, listen carefully to the description of the situation. Discuss with your child what the teacher or principal said. "Mary, Mr. Smith called today. He said you kept getting out of your seat and taking the other children's crayons. Can you tell me what happened?" Help her to recall her actions. She may continue to deny Mr. Smith's allegations. Respond with: "You say that you didn't get out of your seat. Why do you think Mr. Smith would tell me that you did?" Your child may complain that the teacher doesn't like her, always picks on her, lets the other kids get away with the same things she gets in trouble for. There is a slim possibility your child may be right.

Every semester, the students whose names I learn immediately are the ones who get into trouble on the first day. Once I've identified them as troublemakers, I watch them more closely and catch them more often. Teachers aren't any more perfect than parents. There are times when you should take your child's word over the teacher's, but not often.

If what you're hearing from your child's teacher doesn't ring true, request a conference. The three (or four) of you (parents, teacher, and child) should sit down and discuss appropriate classroom behavior. Review what has been happening. Don't attack the teacher, even if he did make a mistake. It's not easy controlling a classroom of thirty-plus youngsters. Accusations will not make life any easier for your child. Instead of: "You're always picking on our kid," try: "I can understand that with so many children in the classroom, you can sometimes accuse the wrong child. In the future Mary promises to behave herself and to not hang around kids who are misbehaving." Give the teacher credit for trying while letting your child know that you believe her. "Mary, I know that you think Mr. Smith is unfair. I think this time he just made a mistake. You can help him by being extra good in class."

Being well-behaved in class doesn't mean never speaking out or calling out an answer. It does mean following the rules, having good manners, and coming to school prepared and on time. On the first day of school, your child walks into the classroom equipped with the behaviors you have taught her. She is a walking advertisement for your parenting skills. Think about it.

MULTICULTURALISM AND DIFFERENCE

Few school communities are completely homogeneous. Most school populations are multicultural and may also include students with different physical capabilities. In order for a classroom environment to be most conducive to learning, a child needs to learn to respect the differences among her peers.

Children are not born racist or prejudiced. These are learned attitudes and behaviors that can devastate a child and severely inhibit her learning potential. Teaching your child to treat people respectfully is important to her well-being, and to the well-being of her fellow students. She will adopt your attitudes and she will apply them at school.

The best way to teach your child is by example. Pay attention to the words you use and the way you act. Don't use insensitive language or racial slang. Think about how your child would feel if such words were directed at her. Teach her to treat people in ways she would like to be treated.

Do talk about the differences between people with your child. By age two she will begin to notice that people are not all the same. A child knows the difference between someone in a wheelchair and someone walking. She can see that the "white" girl looks different from the "brown" girl. Your child is being naturally curious when she asks, "Why can't Mary walk?" or "Why does Samantha have 'funny' eyes?" Don't be afraid of or shy away from sensitive subjects. Your child's curiosity provides the perfect opportunity to teach her about difference without prejudice or hatred.

Even if your home environment is loving, your child may pick up some derogatory words at school or on the playground. Don't be shocked into smacking her or washing her mouth out with soap if she comes home repeating racial slurs. Instead, explain, "Sometimes people say hurtful things. Usually it is because they don't know any better. That is a hurtful word. Now you know better." Or, "Yes, that man's skin looks like chocolate; it's brown. People with brown skin are called African-American or Black."

Don't let a biased remark go by without comment. "It's hurtful when you call people those names. How would you feel if someone talked to you that way?" Talk it through. Discuss the differences. "People come from many different countries. In Asia most people have eyes like Chung's. In Africa most people have dark skin. In Europe many people have white skin. Here we have a mix, so you're right, everyone is not the same. But that doesn't mean it's better to have red hair than blonde hair. Don't judge people by how they look."

If your child comes home upset because she wasn't allowed to participate in a game because of her color or religion, heard kids calling her names, or experienced any form of prejudice, talk about her feelings. "It's hurtful when people say those things or exclude us because of our skin color. It's sad that that little girl didn't learn all of us are different in some ways and alike in others. Your skin (eyes, hair, religion, language) is beautiful. That other child has a problem getting along with people and knowing the difference between right and wrong. You do not."

Suppose your child reports that her teacher made some negative racial remark. Discuss it with the teacher. Find out what the circumstances were before making any assumptions. Your child may or may not have misinterpreted or taken the teacher's words out of context. You might say, "Yesterday, my daughter said she heard you say Hispanic children are not smart. Perhaps she misunderstood what you said. Could you explain what happened?" Then listen. The explanation may be a simple one, or it may not.

Teachers represent a cross section of the country. Unfortunately, some are racist or prejudiced. While we may not be able to stop prejudice, we certainly don't have to condone it in the classroom. A negative environment will affect your child's learning. If the teacher doesn't believe your child can learn, then change teachers. If no other teacher is available, change schools. Do report the teacher to higher authorities. Prejudiced behavior is inexcusable.

THERE ARE SOME LEMONS ON EVERY STAFF

My sister, who taught for twenty years before becoming a school counselor, used to begin her parent meetings with, "I promise not to believe everything your child tells me about you, if you promise not to believe everything your child tells you about me." It's still a good rule of thumb. However, in my years as both a parent and teacher, I have come across several teachers who have been truly abusive to their students. For this reason, it is important that parents listen carefully to what their children are saying.

Abuse by a teacher includes inappropriate or excessive touching. Abuse also includes ridicule, teasing, discrimination, unfairness in grading, unequal treatment of students, and failure to provide meaningful lessons and curricula content.

How will you know if your child's teacher is abusive? By talking to your child. Ask him: "What did you learn at school today?" "What games did you play during recess?" "How did you get along with your teacher(s)?" "Tell me about the bean plant you're growing in science." "What about the stories you read in class?" I'm not suggesting that you go down the list, or even that you make a list of your own. Simply engage your child in meaningful conversation about school daily. Don't allow the conversation to end with, "What did you do in school today?" "Nothing."

Students who know their parents are genuinely interested in what they are doing will be more open and willing to share their school news. It's important to begin the dialog while your child is very young. If you think it's difficult getting information from your young child, I assure you, it's much more difficult to talk to a teenager who is in the habit of keeping to herself. When you frequently discuss school with your child, you're more likely to be aware when there is a change in her attitude or behavior. Be sure to find time for listening.

If you suspect something at school has gone awry, call the school promptly to arrange for a conference with the teacher. Don't insist that the principal be involved at the first meeting—you'll only make the teacher feel defensive. A falsely accused teacher will be doubly sensitive to your child. In the future, he may back away from offering any special assistance, even when your child needs it. Get the facts before you make any accusations. If you don't believe you and your child are being heard, then ask to meet with the principal.

In general, most of the problems a child will have with her teachers will be of a minor nature. During her lifetime, a child will come into contact with hundreds of people, not all of whom she'll like. You can help your child prepare for this reality by encouraging her to discuss what she likes or dislikes about her teachers and how she can best work with them. "Mr. Teacher is always grumpy in the morning. It's not that he doesn't like you. Remember how mean grandpa acted before he had his coffee? Well, your teacher is just like that." "Mrs. Teacher doesn't like a lot of noise in her classroom. Some people are more tolerant of noise than others. You may have to save the giggles until you're on the playground." "I know Mr. Teacher gets really angry when students don't have their homework. He wants you all to be successful and earn good grades. If you have your homework, he won't be angry with you."

Sometimes you can help the teacher. "Mr. Smith, my little Johnny is very frightened because you're so much bigger than he is. Perhaps if you could sometimes bend down when you speak to him, he'll learn how nice you are and not be afraid." "Marie thinks when you yell at the class that you are angry with her. Perhaps you could tell the students why you are angry." You're not being presumptuous in suggesting ways your child's teacher could do a better job. Teachers, just like everyone else, are always trying to grow and improve. Even if they don't follow your suggestion, they will think about it.

Don't share your horror stories about school and teachers with your young children. Inexperienced students are very susceptible. If you went to a school where teachers regularly whipped the students, keep it to yourself for now. When your student complains of a bad teacher, don't tell her about a teacher you had who was even worse. If you had bad school experiences and are therefore down on school, you might transfer your negative attitude to your children without meaning to. Instead, share your positive experiences when possible. If you must repeat the horror stories, water them down. "I didn't get along very well with my third grade teacher. I wish I could have had a different one. I should have tried harder anyway."

Most teachers are in the classroom because they genuinely like kids and believe all children can learn. Everyone benefits when you become a partner with your child's teacher.

GETTING TO KNOW THE SCHOOL

School can be pretty scary for a kid. It is, after all, a big, overwhelming place, and children are very small. They may be frightened by the possibility of getting lost, not being able to find the bathroom and wetting themselves, having a mean teacher, losing their books and supplies, not being liked by other children, getting sick in class, feeling lonesome, or missing you. While you can't possibly wipe out all of your child's school anxieties, planning ahead will help make the transition from home to school a lot less traumatic.

Before your child's first day, visit the school she'll be attending. Most schools have new-student orientation days that include meeting the staff and a tour of the school grounds. Attend with your child. The orientation will give your student an opportu-

nity to become familiar with the school and to meet some of her future classmates while you meet their parents.

In addition to an organized orientation, you may also want to take a self-guided tour of the school with your child. Ask the office for a map to help find the important locations.

If you know in advance who your child's first teacher will be, ask to spend a morning or afternoon in her class. If the teacher assignments haven't been made, you and your child may be able to visit for an hour or two in each of the kindergarten (first grade, etc.) classrooms. The teacher might invite your youngster to participate in an activity. Quietly point out things that are happening in class. Where is the reading center? The science corner? Look at some of the books. Check out the children's art work on the bulletin boards. Note how students raise their hands and wait to be called upon. Remark upon how the teacher acts toward the other children. Visiting school with you is a wonderful opportunity for your child to test her future surroundings without leaving the safety of your companionship.

When you're at the school, introduce your youngster to the adults who will play a prominent role in her life for the next few years. Meet the principal, say hello to the school nurse, visit the custodian. "Hello Mr. Custodian. My daughter Emily will be attending your elementary school in the fall." "Emily, this is Mr. Custodian. He helps to keep the school clean. You can help him by placing your trash in the waste baskets and by cleaning up after yourself when you're in the cafeteria." Explaining each person's function will make the school and staff more familiar to your child, and it will teach her that everyone is important and deserves respect.

If you've taken the time to meet the staff, you and your child will most likely be remembered well when the new term begins. You will have already established yourself as a caring, involved parent and that initial impression will be transferred to your child.

HELPING YOUR CHILD STAND OUT IN A CROWD

In an ideal world, all children would receive the finest education available. They would be exposed to every opportunity possible, and get every chance at success. Unfortunately, many circumstances prevent this from being the case. Large classrooms, inadequate resources, and little community support make it easy for some children to fall through the cracks. Luckily, there are many things you can personally do to help your child receive the attention she deserves.

Establishing regular communication with your child's teacher will greatly benefit your child. At the start of the school year, send a letter to your child's teacher. Introduce yourself and offer your services to the class. Whether you can contribute major supplies, chaperone a class trip, teach a special skill, or save the teacher a few hours by cutting out paper pumpkins for the Halloween party, your efforts will be appreciated. Offering your time and resources will let the teacher know that you are a concerned parent. The reality is that children of parents who volunteer usually get more attention from their teacher. That extra attention can make the difference between getting your child assistance at the very beginning of a problem, or in allowing her to get lost in the crowd.

The following sample letters to the teacher are only offered as suggestions. Think about how much time and money you have to offer, or any special skills you can contribute, and write your letter accordingly.

Dear Teacher:

I am delighted that my daughter, _____, will be in your class this year. I have heard wonderful things about you from other parents. I've included a picture of my daughter and our entire family.

The responsibility of educating our child is one I take seriously. I would like to assist you, if I may. (Include your significant other, if he/she is also available to assist.)

Although I work outside of the home and am unavailable during the day, I can help with class projects by assembling work kits and art supplies. I can provide classroom supplies such as scissors, construction paper, buttons, noodles, etc. My company can also arrange for a class visit to _____, tickets to a concert, or a tour of our _____.

Please call me at (day and evening numbers), or send a note home with my child if there is something I can assist with.

Respectfully,
John Doe, _____'s father

OR

Dear Teacher:

I do not work outside the home and am available to accompany the class on field trips, act as an interpreter in (state language), volunteer in the classroom (list possible dates and times), and help with reading groups, art projects, etc. I have a collection of _____ the kids might enjoy seeing, and my family has a pet _____ I could bring to school.

I'm looking forward to working with you throughout the year.

Respectfully,
Jane Doe, _____'s mother

Once the letter is written and mailed (don't send it with your child—she will most likely have her hands full just getting herself to school on time and doing all the things the teacher expects her to do), don't expect a reply right away. Depending upon how much experience the teacher has, it may take her several weeks to get acquainted with the youngsters and plan activities for the year. If something special comes up, call the teacher and let her know. Offer your assistance throughout the year.

Once school begins do attend Open House and Back to School nights. Get to know all of your child's teachers. Children see parental involvement in school as proof that their education is valued.

Becoming educated is a lifelong, full-time job. You are your child's first teacher and you continue to be your child's teacher throughout her life. Get involved in school. In addition to helping your community, your child will reap the benefits of having an involved parent.

REPORT CARDS AND GRADES

Report cards, sometimes called progress reports, are a teacher's and school's way of recording your child's progress. Don't ignore them. While the grades and comments may not always be 100 percent accurate, they are a good indicator of how your child is doing in school.

Schools usually distribute report cards six or more times during the school year. Know when they are issued. Some schools mail report cards home, some send them home with students. Children who are not progressing well academically or who have misbehaved and fear their behavior has been recorded often find ways to not bring their report card home. If you suspect you have missed a report card, call the school.

In addition to grades, report cards usually list the total number of days a student has been absent or tardy. The most obvious reason for poor academic performance is poor attendance. Sometimes parents don't realize how many days their child has missed; a day here and a day there can add up. If your child misses twenty days a year, she's missed more than ten percent of all instructional time. Your child cannot do well if she's not in school.

When you receive a report card, discuss it with your youngster. Make sure that each of you understands what every mark means. If you don't understand the grading system, arrange for a conference with the teacher. Don't wait until the next report card is issued. For example, if your child is having a problem with reading, organization, or getting to class on time, the sooner you intervene the better. Together with the teacher you can assist your child.

I have mixed feelings about paying students for good grades. On the one hand, the best motivation is inherent: learning is its own reward. A good education can also lead to a better life with more choices and a greater chance at job satisfaction. Yet, these are lofty goals the young child will probably not understand.

Pay, on the other hand, can provide a child with a tangible, identifiable goal. Pay can consist of a special trip or outing if the grades reach a pre-established level. Children can also be rewarded with money they get to spend on things important to them. Research has shown kids respond well to receiving payment for good grades.

While I am unclear about how I feel about rewarding good grades with pay, I think it is extremely important that poor grades and work habits result in a loss of privileges and in more parent-imposed study time. Consider setting up additional reading time, severely restricting TV time, and limiting time spent on computer games or out with friends. Hitting and yelling at your child in response to poor grades seldom produces positive results.

Seek your child's help. Ask, "How can we help you to do better?" "Why do you think your grades were so low?" Don't accept your child's excuse that her teacher does not like her. Instead ask, "Do you turn in your homework every day?" "Do you get to class on time?"

All children can learn. If you expect a lot from your child, offer her lots of encouragement, and help her organize her time productively, she will do well. If you don't know what to do, meet with your child's teacher and work out a plan. Everyone's goal is for your child to be a successful student. Work together toward that goal.

SELF-ASSESSMENT AND SCHOOL PORTFOLIOS

While it is valuable to know the teacher's assessment of your child's performance, children take real ownership of their education when they learn how to assess themselves. Starting a portfolio is a great way for a child to keep track of her own progress and learning.

A portfolio is a collection of work. Many professionals use portfolios. A photographer takes a folder of her photographs on a job interview. A model puts his best pictures in his portfolio. The architect goes to a new client armed with examples of the work she has done before. In many classrooms, students are now required to keep a portfolio.

In its simplest form, a student portfolio contains writing assignments, book reports, drawings, science reports, tests, and other items the teacher and student may consider important. During the school year, the teacher will ask students to periodically reexamine the items in their portfolios. It is an eye-opener when kids compare their current work to that from six months ago. Remarks like "This drawing looks like a baby did it. This is what I can do now," or "I can't believe I made so many spelling mistakes. I know all those words now," are common. Children get excited and inspired by their own progress.

Whether or not your child has a portfolio in school, you can help her develop one at home. All you need to begin is a simple folder and a place to store it. For the preschool child, you may want to save drawings. Let your child select the ones to put into the portfolio. Periodically sort through the pictures together. Some will stay and others will get tossed. As your child gets older and begins to experiment with the alphabet, open a second portfolio for writing. Add folders as your child takes on new challenges.

Your child's portfolios will get more and more sophisticated as she progresses through school. Periodically analyze the contents together. "Remember when you couldn't write your name? Look at how well you write now." "Where else have you seen improvement?" "How did you learn to do that?" "What do you need/want to work on some more?"

Portfolios are also accurate methods of assessing report card grades. "You said your teacher made a mistake on the report card. Let's see if we can find the work she said you didn't complete." Confronted with the reality of her own work, your child will stop thinking in terms of "the teacher doesn't like me" or "the teacher gave me this grade." She'll begin to realize that "this is what I earned." Your child has a greater chance of success if she can recognize her accomplishments and take responsibility for her failures. A portfolio is an easy-to-use method for helping her achieve ownership of her education.

Chapter 7

HOMEWORK

HOMEWORK, the educational work your child does at home, is an integral part of his schooling. During school, the teacher introduces new concepts which the student then reinforces through practice at home. Homework includes reading, writing, and computing. Homework also includes projects such as planting a bean and watching it grow, building a three-dimensional model, and charting the planets on a poster board. Projects are a way for the student to reinforce what he's learned in school and to demonstrate his mastery of the material at hand.

Attendance and homework are the two factors most likely to separate good students from those who are unsuccessful. With very few exceptions, all children can do well in school. Making the honor roll takes regular attendance, attention to what is happening in class, and serious effort during after-school hours. It takes doing homework.

How much homework? For kindergarten and first-grade students, plan on thirty minutes to one hour of homework nightly. Second-, third-, and fourth-graders usually need one to two hours for homework. Time spent on homework varies greatly depending on how much is assigned, the difficulty of the assignment, and how well your child applies himself. The child who hurries through his homework in fifteen minutes is probably not achieving his highest potential.

Occasionally, your child may not have a written homework assignment, but there is always school work for him to do. "You have no homework tonight? Then it's a good time to review the spelling words for Friday's test." "Let's start that new book you wanted to read." "You can write letters to your grandparents about what you've been doing in school and practice your handwriting at the same time." "You can take time to redo some of your papers which are pretty messy." He should be reading, whether assigned or not, a minimum of fifteen minutes nightly.

If your child always says there's no homework and you suspect otherwise, call the teacher and ask. Let your child know that you and the teacher are partners. Calling the teacher is not an attempt to catch your child in a lie, but rather a sincere effort to help him become the best he can be. Homework is an important tool for reinforcing what children are learning in school. It is an essential part of the educational program. Teachers who don't give regular homework may not believe your child can achieve. Such an attitude can be very detrimental to a young child. If the teacher is not giving assignments, I'd ask why not.

Be skeptical if your child always tells you that he did all his homework in school. He may be skipping classwork in order to get the homework done. However, if he can finish the homework while the other students are completing their classwork and his grades are still high, there's a good chance your child is not being sufficiently challenged in his classes. Consult the teacher. Ask: "Can my child receive more advanced work?" "Supplemental materials?" "Extra books to read and report on?" "Can he help teach other students who may be having more difficulty?" You don't want your child to be bored and restless in school because he is not being challenged. If school is too easy, he may soon get turned off to education.

RESPONSIBILITY

It is the teacher's responsibility to assign meaningful homework that reinforces concepts introduced in school. Homework directions should be clearly stated by the teacher, written on the blackboard, or presented in the form of a handout. Completed homework should be collected or otherwise recorded by the teacher. Teachers who never review or correct homework do their students a disservice. If your child tells you he doesn't have to do the homework because the teacher never collects it anyway, call the teacher and ask for his homework policies.

Before leaving school at the end of the day, it is your child's responsibility to make certain that he understands what the homework assignment is, he knows how to do it, and that he has the materials necessary to complete the assignment. Teachers usually require students to copy homework instructions into their notebooks. As a precaution, see that your child has the phone numbers of at least two other classmates.

It is your child's responsibility to do his assignments and to bring them to school when they are due. Students generally do not get credit for "I left my homework on the kitchen table," "My brother took it to school by mistake," or "My mother threw it out when she was cleaning my room." It is crucial that your child get into the habit of doing his homework.

It is not a parent's job to do her child's homework. It is a parent's responsibility to provide a quiet place for her child to study, time for homework, and assistance when necessary. It is a parent's responsibility to ask questions about the assignments and to check that the homework is completed at the highest level of performance her child is capable of.

A QUIET PLACE

A quiet place must be provided for your child to complete his after-school studying. Even if living conditions are cramped, it's important that everyone in the household respect the time set aside for completing homework. If there is no private place for your child to work, then use the kitchen table. Turn off the television and radio. Don't answer the phone. Send the neighbors and their children home. Chores can wait. Save your arguing until later. The place where your child does his homework should be as quiet and peaceful as possible. It is the rare child who can concentrate when all about him is chaos. If there is absolutely no quiet place at home, check out the local library, the community center, or call the school to see if there are after-hours programs.

A child's bedroom may not be the best place for studying. There are too many distractions to keep him from his work. It is too easy for him to listen to music, play with toys, read comic books, talk to his siblings, watch TV, etc. in the comfort of his own room. Besides, you can't supervise if he's in there, and he's not as likely to ask for help if he has to get up and seek you out.

STUDY TIME

I am always amazed and disappointed when parents allow their children to watch two or three hours of television each evening, but don't set aside quiet time for homework. Your child needs regular home-work time every day. If things are hectic, plan ahead. Make sure everyone in the house respects homework time.

With your child's assistance, create a schedule which is both flexible and rigid. It should allow ample time for after-school activities, play, and study, but once the schedule is in place, there should be few exceptions to it. Keep in mind that study time doesn't have to be the same time every day, just so long as there is time set aside for it daily.

Tailor the schedule to your child's specific needs. Some nights he may have more homework than others. Tests are frequently given on Fridays which may mean your child needs more study time on Thursday evenings. Plan accord-ingly. If some after-school activities tire him out so he can't do his homework, eliminate the activities or make time in between for a short nap.

If your child has problems following a reasonable sched-ule, try using the timer to give him a better sense of time. Explain, "When the timer rings, it will be time for you to begin your homework. You may play until then." "When the timer rings, it will be time to hang up the phone (put away your toys, send your friend home, etc.), and do your homework."

Thirty minutes to an hour may seem like an eternity to a young child. Allow for breaks. "You can do your homework for fifteen minutes (set the timer) then take a five-minute break before completing it."

Although every child should contribute to the family by doing his share of chores, don't overload your child. Homework should always come before doing the dishes. A child's principal job is to get an education and to prepare to be a contributing citizen. Children should do their studying while they are still fresh enough to concentrate.

Students who push their homework time until very late risk not learning much. Their minds are just too tired to think clearly. Studying and homework should come first, not last.

Homework time can be a time for the entire family. You can sit around a table, or in the same room, and mom can read the newspaper or complete a report for the office, dad can read his favorite detective story or balance his checkbook, brother and sister can work on their schoolwork. Homework is any work done at home. When the family members each do their homework at the same time, there's an added sense of togetherness. The kids get the message that homework is important and necessary, and not just a punishment because they're kids. Working together also encourages a positive work ethic in your children. It gives them a foundation from which to build success.

Assistance means help. It does not mean that parents should do their children's homework—projects and reports included. You can help your child with his homework by setting aside a quiet time and a comfortable place for him to study, and by being available to help him work through what he does not understand.

Providing your child with all the materials he needs to complete his work is also important. Every home should have a supply of paper, pens, pencils, a pencil sharpener, a good-quality dictionary, and, if possible, a set of encyclopedias or a CD-ROM encyclopedia for reference.

Before beginning his homework, ask your child to tell you what he's going to do, and how he plans to go about doing it. If he says something you don't understand or you suspect he's not exactly clear what the assignment involves, ask him to explain it more clearly. Verbalizing the assignment can help to clarify it.

Once both you and your child understand the assignment, it is time for him to get to work.

Being in the same room with you may be all the assistance he needs. I used to love doing my homework at the kitchen table while my mother prepared dinner. I could tell her what I was doing, read passages to her, and still get my work done.

You don't have to be able to do the work yourself to be of assistance to your child. Ask him to explain what he's doing and to teach you how to do it. Lots of young children, natural sponges for absorbing second languages, teach their nonnative-born parents how to speak English. Having to explain something to you will reinforce your child's mastery of the subject, raise his self-esteem, and possibly teach you something new.

Check your child's work over before he quits for the evening. If the assignment called for ten math problems, make sure he completed ten. Ask what the criteria were for the written composition and then check his work against them. If the work is messy, require him to copy it over more neatly.

Pride in what your child accomplishes translates into a strong work ethic. Whether he's doing homework or chores, if you condone sloppy or incomplete work, that's what he'll do. Honor students, just like workers who rise to the top of their professions, are those with strong work ethics; they apply themselves completely to whatever task they tackle.

Chapter 8

MULTIMEDIA

OUR CHILDREN'S LIVES are immersed in electronics. Television is a regular part of life for most kids and movies have become standard weekly entertainment. The bleep of a computer or video game can be heard almost everywhere a kid is to be seen, and for most, life cannot even be fathomed without the background hum of a radio or CD player. Yet most of us don't even notice. These things are a normal part of our lives, too.

Television, movies, computers, video games, and radio are powerful mediums that can have lasting effects, both negative and positive, on our children. As a parent, it is not only your right, it is your responsibility to monitor and control your child's access to them.

TELEVISION

Enough has been written about the negative aspects of television to fill ten volumes. We know that programs with violent content desensitize our children to real-life violence. Solving conflicts through force, as so many television programs do, teaches our children that the strongest person wins. Foul language on the airwaves brings foul language into our homes. Images of women as beautiful but submissive still abound, affecting young girls' self-esteem and problems with body image. There is no question that the influential power of television is immense.

You've probably already heard all of these criticisms and more about television. Yet the problem with TV is only partially in the programs aired. TV is passive entertainment. It trains children to expect mental stimulation to come from outside of themselves. It teaches a child to expect someone or something to entertain her. It encourages her to forget about the possibilities that lay within her own imagination.

Once your child sits in front of the set, even if she is watching an educational program, she is a passive observer. The show continues when she leaves the room to raid the refrigerator or to play with a toy. If she's confused over something she's watching, the television program doesn't stop to clarify.

Watching television teaches your child that she doesn't have to think. When the director wants the viewer to pay attention to something specific, the camera goes in for a close-up. The viewer is not expected to search the screen for meaningful details or actors' expressions. Close-ups take care of the subtleties.

Shows like *Barney* and *Sesame Street* can teach children about numbers and getting along with their playmates, but they are still a passive activity. Kids' shows tend to be very stimulating with a multitude of color, graphics, and sounds. The action and colors on the screen change so rapidly (once every three or four seconds) that the child's attention span becomes very limited. Researchers are already linking the rise in attention deficit disorder to excessive television viewing. Children who watch a lot of television report being bored more often than children who do not rely on the television for entertainment.

On the average, children spend more hours per week watching television than they spend in school. They spend more time watching TV each evening than on homework. The same child who can recite all the characters in all the afternoon shows, or the one who regularly tapes the shows she misses for later viewing, often can't remember what she did in school that day or what she's expected to do for homework.

One year I asked a group of elementary students to draw pictures of themselves and/or family members watching television. I wish I had kept those drawings which showed listless, expressionless faces flanked by large bowls of popcorn and other snacks, bottles of beer, cigarettes, and, in one drawing, a person yelling at another to "shut up." That's how kids see themselves and their families when they watch TV.

Now, place those same students in a classroom setting. Listless behavior, an inability to follow directions, lack of organization, and restlessness are commonplace. They keep their eyes down to become invisible and avoid teacher contact. They constantly complain of being bored. They are a sharp contrast to the successful students in the room. The successful students are engaged in what they are doing. They don't view education as a passive process.

Watching television takes time and is addictive. Programmers know it is difficult to watch just one show. They preview upcoming programs with commercial spots: "Stay tuned for more. . . ." It's difficult for a child to tell herself, "That's enough," and then turn off the tube. More time in front of the TV means less time spent in meaningful activity, play, interacting with parents, and physical movement.

time
out

Many children are addicted to television. They cannot seem to be satisfied unless the TV is on. An addicted child may make up reasons why she can't go to school. She'd rather stay home and watch television than do schoolwork. To break the habit, turn off the set, especially on days when she's too "ill" to attend school.

If your child is doing poorly in school, the first step is to limit her television time and to remove the TV set from her room. There is a very high correlation between children who do poorly in school, and children who have a television in their bedroom or are left unattended with the television as a baby-sitter. After a lot of complaining and even some serious withdrawal symptoms, your child may begin to pay more attention to her schoolwork. It's not a magic solution, but without the TV to turn to, she may be bored enough to do her homework.

There aren't too many things I feel strongly enough about to guarantee, but I assure you that if there is no television in your child's room and you limit her TV time to thirty minutes per evening, you are helping her achieve success. If you're not yet convinced, think of what happens when you read. Reading requires your attention, involvement, and interaction. If your mind wanders when you're reading, you go back and reread. Television, on the other hand, requires nothing. Whether you understand or not, the television show moves along without you. That's how life goes for the child who comes to school saturated with television viewing. Her education moves along without her.

Are there exceptions? Can your child make an argument for passing classes and still watching television? Certainly. But just to be sure, I would advise restricting TV time anyway.

TV Rules of Thumb

◆ No television sets in a child's room.

◆ Do not use the TV as a baby-sitter.

◆ Limit TV to half an hour on school nights and one hour on non-school nights.

◆ Pre-select the show(s) your child will watch. If there is an exceptional show, tape it for later when you can eliminate the commercials and watch it together.

◆ Whenever possible, join your kids for TV time. Watching together allows you to discuss the show's content.

MOVIES AND VIDEOS   Nearly every student I know has a home video library. Even though videos are expensive (they usually cost more than books), it is not unusual for many students to have dozens of videos in their homes. These same students often own no books. Parents think they are helping their children by purchasing videos the kids can watch over and over again. But watching videos can be as detrimental as watching TV. After all, your child watches videos on a television screen.

Besides being a passive activity, movies can have great impact on your child's values and goals. Consider this message: Don't work, steal the food and things you want, don't go to school, run away from the authorities, then marry someone rich. Are those the values you want to teach your children? Probably not. Yet, this is Disney's version of *Aladdin*, one of the top-selling children's films.

How about this one? Stepmothers and stepsisters are wicked. Good things happen to us when we wish for them, not when we work for them. The most important trait for a young woman is to be beautiful, because then a man will come along to make her happy. Is that the message you want your daughters to receive? If it is, *Cinderella* is the movie for you.

I could continue, but you get the idea. Do pay attention to what your youngsters watch. Sure, Disney films are entertaining, colorful, and have charming characters, but they also have story lines and express values which you may find, upon reflection, not in line with your family's.

Children are very impressionable. Messages, even subliminal ones, that are repeated over and over can impact them tremendously. If your child must (although I can't imagine why) watch films which promote questionable values, take the opportunity to discuss their content. Compare the values displayed in the films with the values your family lives by.

In addition to the values being promoted, parents should

pay attention to the emotions movies may invoke in their youngsters. Entertainment should not be traumatic. In November 1996, when Mel Gibson's film *Ransom* was released, my husband and I went to see it on opening day. A young couple with two children, ages two and six, was seated next to us in the theater. I couldn't pay much attention to the movie because I kept thinking about these two kids watching a child on screen being kidnapped, handcuffed, chained, blindfolded with duct tape, threatened with a knife and a gun, bloodied, and left alone in a darkened room. Undoubtedly those children came away from their "family outing" fearful for their own safety. Parents' assurances of "It's only a movie" usually do not wash away a child's nightmares.

Next time the family is thinking of going to the movies, consider going to the library or a bookstore instead. Libraries are free and relaxing. Bookstores offer story hours, lots of book choices, comfortable chairs to begin your reading, and opportunities to hear an author present original work. Sometimes there's even a coffee bar for added pleasure. Libraries and bookstores are user-friendly places where patrons generally exhibit good manners, speak gently to one another, and are engaged in intelligent activity—all traits, in addition to being literate, that are desirable for the successful child.

Contrast a library or bookstore visit with going to the movies. A family of four will spend over $22.00 admission for a show lasting less than two hours. Parents will be harassed by children into buying high-priced, high-calorie treats. Most films have violent content, foul language, and adult scenes. Plus, sitting silently in a theater is not an activity that allows the family to have quality, interactive time together. It will be an expensive outing with little positive outcome.

If you do go to the movies or send your kids without you, pay attention to what they'll be viewing. Most newspapers contain short summaries of current films. Read them, check the movie ratings, and select carefully.

RADIO

Music is enticing. It floods our heads with its rhythms and sounds. It can soothe us and help us relax. But our brains can only focus on so much. If our brains are filled with music, then they are not filled with something else, like thought.

Soft background music, especially classical Baroque, is soothing and, according to recent research, can stimulate the brain. Loud music and constant racket do the opposite. An incessantly blaring radio can wipe out the quiet time your child needs for thinking. If the radio is always going, concentrated reflection is not happening. Chances are if your family is dependent on having a radio or TV playing nonstop in the background, there's not much communication happening between family members.

Headsets are a more serious problem. Besides causing hearing damage, listening to music (or anything else) through a headset effectively cuts off any outside conversation and internal imagination. The blaring, intense noise, be it music or speech, knocks out the opportunity for thought. Kids walk around with headsets on so they don't have to think. Children who are successful in school spend time thinking. Often solutions to current problems, replays of lessons, and thoughts about relationships are bouncing around in a child's head. Headsets blaring loud music can cut off necessary quiet time.

I'm not proposing you toss out the radio, but do consider monitoring it. Children, like all of us, need quiet time to think.

HOME COMPUTERS

To be successful in the 21st century, your child needs to be computer literate. While some school districts are making great progress in providing computer classes for all of their students, most schools are moving forward at a snail's pace.

As opposed as I am to using credit cards to finance purchases that cannot be afforded, I make an exception for home computers. Every child should have access to a home computer as soon as she enters school, and even before. Consider combining all of the family holiday and birthday gifts to purchase a computer for everyone to use.

Your child does not need to have her own computer, tucked into a corner of her bedroom, inaccessible to other family members. Nor does she need the latest in technology. For starters, a used computer purchased at a swap meet will do. Because computer technology is constantly advancing, prices drop drastically and quickly. Last year's computer models often sell for less than half of their original price and are probably more than adequate for your family's needs.

If you prefer to purchase new, before you go to a computer store, think about how your family will use its computer. Do you want a good word processor? Are you interested in charting stocks and bonds? Is sending e-mail and faxes a priority? Are you interested in designing your own greeting cards? Knowledgeable clerks in a computer store can be very helpful. If you're thoroughly confused, call your child's school and ask to speak with someone who is computer literate. Every school has personnel who love talking about computers and will be willing to assist you in making a good selection.

Don't know much about using a computer? Again, use the neighborhood school as a resource. Call the high school and tell them you are willing to pay a knowledgeable student to tutor your family in using the computer. Some of the best computer teachers I know are high school students. With their help, you can enjoy private tutoring in your home for only a small hourly fee.

If at all possible, purchase a computer capable of hooking up to the Internet. The Internet is an extensive source of information. It offers access to past and present data and current research on an unlimited range of subjects. Furthermore, the student who knows how to access the Internet, obtain needed information, assess that information, and combine the Internet data with data obtained from other sources, will be far more ready for the demands of college and the workplace.

Caution: the Internet is time-consuming, enticing, and filled with as much useless information as helpful data. Losing one's complete sense of time as one traverses web sites is a real possibility. It's as necessary to monitor a child's computer time as it is her TV time.

To guard against your child coming across questionable or obscene content on the Internet, establish strict rules for the kinds of sites she may explore, and stay nearby as she does her "surfing." You may want to talk ahead of time about the goal of an Internet session and keep your child on task as she tracks down information on dinosaurs, a foreign country, birdwatching, etc.

Since the 1950s, when families first began to acquire television sets, the sets became the focal point of the family's living quarters. With the 21st century approaching, it's time to move the TVs aside and focus on the computer. The computer should be located where the entire family will have access. Learning together, sharing information and excitement over learning, and even playing computer games together are some of the benefits. But sharing a computer is also practical and economical: it removes the necessity of duplicating equipment.

Another benefit of sharing the computer is supervision. Computers can be as addictive as television. Kids go into their bedrooms, log onto their computers, and play computer games or "surf the net" for hours—often to the detriment of their schoolwork. I'm not aware of any truly effective way to monitor your child's computer time if she's tucked away in her bedroom. Centrally locating and sharing the computer will prevent any one person from monopolizing it. Siblings and parents, wanting their turn at the keyboard, won't let anyone stay on for too long. If that doesn't work, you can make sure everyone gets a chance by allocating them time slots. Be flexible, use the timer if you have to, and remember that schoolwork should always have precedence over almost everything else.

Educational software is also a valuable benefit of owning a computer. Young children can benefit from games which teach them to recognize words, sounds, colors, string words into sentences, and even write simple stories with illustrations. When choosing software, make your selections carefully. Knowledgeable salespeople can assist you with your choices, as can other parents, librarians, teachers, or day care personnel. Stores specializing in educational toys are also a wonderful resource, as are many books and catalogs that highlight educational software. As with other things you purchase for your children, read the labels carefully. Ask, "How will my child benefit from this product?"

It's not too soon to introduce your child to a computer. When children begin early they are comfortable with the technology, able and willing to experiment, and can teach themselves about advanced computer use. Computer literacy will be a necessary component of being educated in the 21st century. By third grade a computer literate child knows the keyboard and can access a variety of computer programs. You can get your child off to a head start by providing computer access.

VIDEO AND COMPUTER GAMES

Video and computer games can be addictive. The loud noises and intense graphics are fascinating. Even simple games such as "Tetris" and "Solitaire" can eat away hours of time and throw responsibility out the window. I often found myself saying, "just one more game" until my playing hand went numb and the clock struck 2 a.m.—and I'm a fairly self-disciplined adult! I finally had to delete all the games from my computer in order to start going to bed at a reasonable hour.

Besides wasting too much time, computer and video games can also be violent. Warriors blow up their enemies, female characters are attired in skimpy garments, and force too often wins over intelligence. Some games have all of the negative characteristics of the worst in television and movies.

You can refuse to purchase violent games for your children—even the boys. Locating the computer where you can keep an eye on it will make it easier to monitor playing time. Not giving your children an endless supply of quarters to sink into the arcade will also help. You can't watch your children every second of the day, however. The best thing to do is to teach your child that rules are rules. Then set up some reasonable parameters and stick to them.

Chapter 9

OUTINGS, TRIPS, AND ADVENTURES

ONE OF MY MOST exciting moments as a grandmother was watching my ten-month-old granddaughter let loose on the lawn for the first time. She rubbed her hands over the grass, crushed it in her fingers, tasted it, put her face close to the ground, and peered intensely. At that moment, she was an explorer discovering uncharted lands.

Children are naturally curious. Everything is new and exciting to them. Exploring an empty tissue box, or a full one, can hold as much adventure as the most expensive infant toy on the market. It is only when a child's curiosity is crushed by: "Don't touch," "I'm tired of your questions," or "Not now," that he stops asking and eventually stops wondering.

As a parent, it is your job to encourage and help your child explore the world around him. A diversity of experiences is key to a rich education. Outings, trips, and adventures can provide exciting opportunities for you and your child to explore and learn about the world together.

Whether you travel to a foreign land or go to an exotic restaurant for dinner, exposure to different cultures, ideas, and activities will excite your child's imagination, and push him to question and discover the world around him.

Plan lots of outings with your child. Begin with your house or apartment, the street you live on, or the store a block away. What may be ordinary to you (row after row of trees or garbage cans, a flock of pigeons, etc.) may be new and extraordinary to your child. Move on to explore your neighborhood or city. Draw maps illustrating the routes you take to the library or store (large sheets of construction paper are great for map drawing). Draw pictures, identify shops and friends' homes, and take photos to put on the maps. Help make the area familiar for your child.

Trips and adventures are not reserved just for school or exotic locations. They can include trips to the backyard, to grandma's, the zoo or museum, the library, the local elementary school your child will eventually attend, or an airplane trip across the country. You can pick cherries, have a picnic, build a fire on the beach, walk in a tunnel, float in a stream, or plant a garden. Trips can be short fifteen-minute excursions or two-week affairs. What makes an outing work is the appropriateness of the trip, the preparation beforehand, and the discussion afterwards. The amount of money you spend is not a measure of success.

By the time your child turns two, you can begin to plan trips together. If you're going to the grocery store, discuss who and what you might see (the check-out clerks, fruit and vegetables), how you're going to get there (by stroller, car, or bus), what you're going to do (shop for groceries), and when you're going to do it. (Even if your child doesn't know how to tell time, he'll understand if you say, "We're

going to the grocery store after breakfast. We'll be home in time for your morning nap.") Plan and write the shopping list together. Have him write his own list—most likely a bunch of squiggled lines on a paper—and tuck it into his pocket to take along.

Upon your return, recall the sequence of events which took place. Talk about what you did first, next, and last. Predicting and recalling are important skills for getting ready to read.

Make sure the excursion you plan is appropriate for your child. A trip which extends to the point of crankiness will not be remembered as a good experience—by you or him. A whole day at Disneyland or a huge street fair can be over-stimulating for a preschooler. An overly long car ride, without stops to throw a frisbee or run through a highway rest area, may take all the excitement out of a trip to grandma's. Consider your child's age, schedule, and stamina, then plan trips which are not too demanding of his energy or his attention.

As much as children crave new experiences, they love familiarity. They live in a world which is constantly changing to them. Being around the familiar helps a child feel more in control. Hence, the child who wants the same story read to him night after night. Be patient when your child wants to revisit the same places over and over. Try to mix new experiences with familiar ones.

Learning to live with pre-set limits is also an important part of an adventure or outing. Kids, just like the rest of us, must learn to take into account the realities of time, money, etc. when having fun. You can set time limits by explaining, "We can only stay at the park one hour. When the little hand is on the four we have to go home." Setting monetary limits can be just as simple. "I have two dollars for treats. You can decide how you want to spend it, but when it's gone there will be no more." Setting limits in advance will help to avoid confrontations later. "Remember how we said there would be two dollars for treats? You chose to use yours early. Perhaps next time you'll do it differently."

Stick to your pre-set limits. Once you start making exceptions, you'll send the message that your pre-set limits aren't limits at all. My son's collections (he loved to collect everything and anything) threatened to overtake our house. I quickly discovered that setting limits in advance was the only way to keep things under control. In a similar situation you might explain, "We're going to go to the beach. There will be lots of things to see, and lots of sea shells and other things you may want to have. You may collect what fits in this basket (small box, envelope, paper or plastic bag)." Your child will have to make tough decisions about what to keep and what to discard. Be firm: "I'm so sorry. That piece of driftwood is very lovely, but your basket is full. You'll have to leave it here."

Teaching your child to accept limitations will help him adjust to school better. His teacher will also only have so much time, space, and supplies allocated for a particular activity. The child who enters school without ever having dealt with limits may become very unhappy and easily frustrated with school.

When you go on an outing with your child, don't be upset if your agendas are different. You may love to watch the antics of the monkeys at the zoo, but your child may prefer the stillness of the snakes. Instead of trying to force your interests onto your child, follow his lead. After all, "being still as a snake" may be a great way to get him to settle down for a nap.

Provide a variety of experiences. With few exceptions, your children will voice support for the things you want to do—that's how much they want your approval. You may love fishing and prefer to stand thigh-deep in a running stream every weekend, but consider taking time to visit a museum, walk through a sculpture garden, or go hear a storyteller with your child. Allowing children to explore and encouraging them to follow their interests, not yours, opens them to learning. Left to judge on his own, your child may surprise you with what he enjoys.

Children who have not had a wide variety of experiences

tend to be quicker to judge and more closed to learning new subjects in school. Trying new things, even if it's just playing a different game or reading a difficult book, involves taking risks. After all, he may not be too good at it. But children who have been exposed to different activities already know that the worst that could happen is usually not so bad. They are more apt to take on new challenges.

It's difficult to excite a child to study history and geography if he's never been out of the neighborhood. Studying world cultures is less appealing if you're always surrounded by people who look and act just like you. If you've never been to an art museum, seen a play performed, or listened to a live concert, then your world is limited. We learn by adding the new to what we already know.

Outings and trips are a wonderful opportunity for a family to open new vistas together. It doesn't matter if seeing Shakespearean dialogue performed, looking at the bold colors of a Diego Rivera painting, or even trying to catch a trout are first-time experiences for you. Learning alongside your child can be thrilling. Besides, children are a great excuse to ride the merry-go-round for the first time. And while you're there, reach for the brass ring.

CONCLUSION

IN LOOKING BACK over the years I spent raising my children, it's hard not to remember everything (well, almost everything) fondly. As our children grew up, my husband and I faithfully attended hundreds of open house events, ballet performances, and oral presentations. I baked tons of cookies, put dozens of gold fish into plastic bags for PTA fund raisers, and spent hours getting freshly-spun cotton candy out of my hair after volunteering at school carnivals. My husband and I often reminisce about all the nights when our kids used to snuggle into our bed to talk about what was troubling them (they seemed to have an uncanny knack for choosing nights when we were feeling amorous toward one another). We still can't believe how quickly they went from elementary school to college, then on to establish their own homes and careers. The years seem to have passed overnight, and my husband and I still can't believe we're now the proud parents of *grown-ups*.

I know that raising children in the '90s and beyond is not the same as it was in the '40s and '50s when I was a child, or in the '70s and '80s when my children were growing up. But even though my brood is grown, as a full-time teacher I work with children every day. I see their struggles and their successes. I talk with them about their problems and their talents. I meet their proud, loving, and often frustrated parents. And I still, despite all the ins and outs of each day, year, or decade, have hope that each and every one of them will become a well-educated, independent, and responsible adult who is content with her life.

Although each child represents a unique challenge and will respond to some techniques and activities more than to others, the advice in this book readily applies to most children. Kids are amazingly resilient; they will survive your faults, and most of their own. Do the very best you can, reflect frequently on how your children are doing, and always encourage and work towards their success. Continue to do whatever works well for you and your child, and don't worry about the rest. Most of all, don't forget to enjoy parenting— I guarantee it is the best, most rewarding adventure you'll ever have.

I'd love to hear how these techniques have worked for you, or any ideas you may have. Send comments and suggestions to:

Adrienne Mack
c/o McBooks Press
120 West State Street
Ithaca, NY 14850
or e-mail: mcbooks@mcbooks.com

RECOMMENDED READING

THE FOLLOWING reading materials contain many valuable suggestions on raising children. Although this short list is far from complete, I have tried to include a variety of sources which offer different ideas and activities. However, be confident enough in your own parenting skills to question what you read, even advice from the so-called experts. Use ideas that make sense to you, and don't worry about the rest.

MAGAZINES

Magazine articles are generally short and easy to read. They can offer little refreshers, helpful insights, and even empathy with what you might be experiencing as you parent. I found these magazines to be the most consistently thoughtful and useful:

Child (110 Fifth Avenue, New York, NY 20022) offers helpful regular features on health, family, and child development.

Family Circle (110 Fifth Avenue, New York, NY 20022) features a small section on parenting issues worth searching out amidst the recipes, crafts, and home fashions.

Family Life (P.O. Box 52220, Boulder, CO 80322-2220) has a little bit of everything. Check it out for some family trip ideas, craft projects, and thoughts on home schooling.

Parenting (1325 Sixth Avenue, New York, NY 10019) covers a wide range of topics from discipline to helping your toddler gain independence. Focus is on younger children.

Parents (685 Third Avenue, New York, NY 10017) features many helpful articles for raising kids, and for keeping your sanity while doing it.

BOOKS

General Reading

Books, as always, are a great resource. Here are some of my favorites:

The Book of Virtues by William Bennett (Simon & Schuster, 1994) supplies a host of mini lessons on the value of living a moral life. Bennett emphasizes living according to the spiritual and governmental laws of the land, and supporting one's community.

Couch Potato Kids: Teaching Kids to Turn Off the TV and Tune Into Fun by Lee Canter and Marlene Canter (National Books, 1996) is the book to try if you're having trouble getting your kids to watch less TV. The authors offer plenty of suggestions for limiting TV time, becoming a critical viewer, and for providing distractions and alternate activities.

It Takes A Village and Other Lessons Children Teach Us by Hillary Clinton (Simon & Schuster, 1996) presents a good overall philosophy about raising kids, their importance in our society, and in our lives.

Wonderful Ways To Love A Child by Judy Ford (Conari Press, 1995) is the perfect refresher for those times when you can't remember why you became a parent. Just open to any page and feel better.

Activity and Educational Resource Books

Wait! Before you plop your children in front of the TV set because you can't think of another activity to keep them occupied, try the following:

Extraordinary Play With Ordinary Things by Barbara Sher (Adams, 1994) is filled with lots of creative ideas for fun. Ms. Sher shows you how to turn milk cartons into building blocks, suggests 35 ways to play with discarded cardboard boxes, and features another 27 games to play with unmatched socks.

Fun Time, Family Time by Susan K. Perry, Andrea Chesman and Sandra Forrest (Avon, 1996). Includes over 700 innovative ways parents and children can spend time playing, laughing, and making memories together.

Games For Writing: Playful Ways to Help Your Child Learn to Write by Peggy Kaye (Farrar, Straus & Giroux, 1995). This series is worth exploring. It includes plenty of great games for math and reading.

100's of Free Things for Kids: Great Stuff You Can Get for Free or Less Than Five Dollars by Dawn Hardy (Signet, 1997). In addition to receiving lots of free stuff, writing to companies is a wonderful way to get your child in the habit of writing.

Playing Smart: A Parent's Guide to Enriching, Offbeat Learning Activities for Ages 4 to 14 by Susan K. Perry (Free Spirit, 1990). This is a great guide to fun and interesting activities.

Raising Curious Kids: Over 100 Simple Activities to Develop Your Child's Imagination by Nancy Sokol Green (Crown, 1995) contains hands-on creative thinking activities and over 600 thought-provoking questions perfect for quiet time.

The Read-Aloud Handbook by Jim Trelease (Penguin, 1995). Don't know what to do when the TV's off? This book offers great suggestions on reading to your children.

Ready, Set, Read and Write; Ready, Set, Count by Marlene Barron (John Wiley & Sons, 1995). This two-volume set contains 180 learning activities for you and your child. Each book is sold separately.

The Sick-in-Bed Book by Meredith Brokaw and Annie Gilbar (Simon & Schuster, 1993) is perfect for those days when your child is just too sick to go to school or out to play. Filled with lots of ideas for quiet play, it will help your child pass the time as he gets better.

What Your (First–Sixth) Grader Needs to Know: Fundamentals of a Good (First–Sixth) Grade Education ed. by E.D. Hirsch, Jr. (Doubleday, 1993). This series has lots of useful information for parents who wish to closely follow what their youngster is being taught in school. Available in both hard and paperback editions, a separate book is devoted to each grade.

INDEX

A

Addition, 78, 80

Alphabet, learning of, 57

Anger, of parent, 23, 29-30, 31

Artwork, 70-72

Attendance, at school, 88-92, 106, 109

Attention, from parent, 26

Attention span, 15, 21, 117

B

Bedtime, 48-49

Behavior
  matching discipline to, 29
  rewarding good, 25, 26
  at school, 93-96

Books
  age appropriate, 63-64
  making your own, 67-68
  recommended, 58, 79, 137-139
  selecting, 61-64
  stores for, 63, 122-123

Boundaries, setting, 25, 26
  See also Limits, setting

Breakfast, 19, 87

Bullies, 43-44

C

Caregiver. *See* Child care

Child care
  knowing what happens at, 38-39

questions to ask about, 37-39

selecting, 37-38

Children
  experimentation of, 15
  independence of, 16-17
  nature of, 14-17
  selfishness of, 15-16
  separation of quarreling, 31
  talking of, 15

Chores, 40-42, 113
  age appropriate, 41-42

Clay, 70

Clothing, for school, 50, 87

Community service, 36

Computers, 124-128
  benefits of sharing, 125-127
  games for, 127, 128
  importance of, 55, 69, 124
  learning to use, 125
  purchasing, 124-125

Consequences, of actions, 30, 34

Consistency, 25, 26-27, 32

Conversation. *See* Talking

Counting, 77-78

Crayons, 70-71

D

Dinner, 19-22

Disappointment, coping with, 33-34

Discipline, 24-30
  basic rules of, 25

Drawing, 70–71

E
Emergency information, 92–93
Expectations
    having reasonable, 25, 27–28
    of success, 34
Experimentation, of children, 15

F
Fairness, 25, 27
Family, definition of, 20
Fine motor skills, 70–72, 73
Finger painting, 70

G
Games, 42–44
    for computers, 127, 128
    for reading, 66–68
    video, 128
Grades, 105–107
    payment for, 106
    portfolio assessment of, 108
    See also Report cards

H
Hand-eye coordination, 17, 70, 73
Headsets, 123–124
Homework, 79, 109–115
    assistance with, 51–52, 65–66, 74, 79–80, 81, 115
    help remembering, 50–51
    place for, 112
    portfolio for, 107–108
    responsibility for, 111–112
    time for, 112–115

I
Illness, and school, 89–92
Independence, of children, 16–17
Internet, 55, 125–126

K
Kennedy, Rose, 21
Kindness, 35–36

L
Language
    development of, 57–58, 69–70
    exposure to, 37, 56, 57–58
    inappropriate, 93–94
    See also Words
Letter writing
    as writing exercise, 75
    of parent to school, 103–105
Libraries, 62, 122
Limits, setting, 22, 132–133
    See also Boundaries, setting
Listening, 22
Literacy programs, 56
Love, 17–19
    and school, 86–87
    suggestions for showing, 18–19

M
Manners, 34–35
Math, 76–82
    activities, 81–82
    at home, 76–79
    and music, 14–15
    parent's attitude toward, 76, 80
    in school, 79, 81
Mealtime
    and communication, 19–23
    tips for, 20–21
Movies, 120–123
Multiculturalism, 96–98
Multiplication, 81, 82
Music, 14–15, 123–124

N
Name, writing of, 72

O

One Fish, Two Fish (Seuss), 79
Organization
    importance of, 46–47
    of library books, 62
    of school work, 50–52
    of time, 47–49
    See also Routine
Outings, 129–134
    ideas for, 130
    importance of, 129–130, 131, 134
    selecting age-appropriate, 131–132
    setting limits for, 132–133

P

Parent
    definition of, 9
    as example, 13–14, 25, 86, 96
    and homework, 111–112, 114–115
    involvement of, at school, 103–105
    and organization, 47
    responsibilities of, 37, 86–88, 111–112, 116
Playmates
    getting along with, 42–44
    sharing with, 35–36
Playtime, 16, 44–45
    tips for, 36, 45
Portfolios, of school work, 107–108
Prejudice, 96–98
Privacy, 16, 23–24
Progress reports. *See* Report cards
Projects
    to develop math skills, 81–82
    to encourage reading, 66–68
    to encourage writing, 69–73
    for school, 51–52

Promises, 33

Q

Questions
    encouraging children to ask, 58
    loaded, 32–33

R

Radio, 123–124
Reading, 23, 55–68
    by child, 66, 110
    to child, 56, 58–61
    parent's attitude toward, 55–56
    projects that encourage, 66–68
    in school, 64–66
    selecting, 61–64
    See also Books
Report cards, 105–107
Respect, 23–24
Responsibilities
    and chores, 40–42, 113
    and homework, 50–52, 111–112, 116
    of parent, 37, 86–88, 111–112, 116
Routine, 47–48, 52
    for bedtime, 48–49
    for homework, 113
    See also Organization
Rules
    explaining reasons for, 25, 28–29
    of teacher, 94–96
    See also Discipline

S

Schedules, 47–48, 112–113
    See also Routine
School, 85–108
    attendance at, 88–92, 106, 109
    behavior at, 93–96
    and grades, 105–107

introducing child to, 101–103
math in, 79–81
portfolio of work from, 107–108
preparation for, 86–88
reading in, 64–66
supplies for, 52, 87–88
volunteering at, 103–105
writing in, 73–74
Selfishness, of children, 15–16
    See also Sharing
Sequencing, 23, 59–60, 131
Set theory, 78, 82
Sharing, 35–36
of computer, 126–127
Siblings
comparing, 33
individual affectionate gestures
for, 18
Social issues, 63
Socialization, 33, 42–44
Stories, creating of, 72–73, 75
Subtraction, 78
Success, definition of, 9
Supplies, for school, 52, 87–88

T
Talking
of children, 15
at mealtimes, 19–23
Teachers, 43–44
and homework, 110, 111
parent's letters to, 103–105
prejudice of, 97–98
problems with, 97–101
rules of, 94–96
Teenagers, 22
Television
negative effects of, 38, 116–120
rules for, 20, 49, 120
and school, 119

Tell Me Why series, 58
Time-outs, 30–32
Toys, 44–45
Trips, 129–134
    See also Outings, Vacations
Trust, 24–25, 33

U
Uniforms, 50

V
Vacations, 91–92
    See also Outings, Trips
Video games, 128
Videos, 120–123

W
Words
best avoided, 32–34
magic, 34–35
    See also Language
Writing, 23, 69–75
preparing for, 69–73
projects that encourage, 69–73,
75
in school, 73–74